THE SELF-MANAGEMENT PSYCHOLOGY SERIES
Carl E. Thoresen, Ph.D., *General Editor*
Stanford University

This series of self-help books presents techniques that really work based on scientifically sound research.

Designed with the layman in mind, each book presents a step-by-step method you can readily apply to solve real problems you confront in everyday life. Each is written by a respected behavioral scientist who has achieved success in applying these same techniques.

BRIAN G. DANAHER is currently a post-doctoral fellow in the Stanford University School of Medicine's Heart Disease Prevention Program.

EDWARD LICHTENSTEIN is a professor of psychology in the Clinical Program at the University of Oregon.

BOOKS IN THE SERIES

Becoming Orgasmic: A Sexual Growth Program for Women,
by Julia Heiman, Leslie LoPiccolo, and Joseph LoPiccolo
Become an Ex-Smoker,
by Brian G. Danaher and Edward Lichtenstein
Don't Be Afraid: A Program for Overcoming Fears and Phobias,
by Gerald Rosen
How to Control Your Drinking,
by William R. Miller and Ricardo F. Muñoz
How to Sleep Better: A Drug-Free Program for Overcoming Insomnia,
by Thomas J. Coates and Carl E. Thoresen
Take It Off and Keep It Off:
A Behavioral Program for Weight Loss and Exercise,
by D. Balfour Jeffrey and Roger C. Katz

Become an Ex-Smoker

Brian G. Danaher

Edward Lichtenstein

A SPECTRUM BOOK

PRENTICE-HALL, INC., *Englewood Cliffs, New Jersey 07632*

Library of Congress Cataloging in Publication Data

DANAHER, BRIAN G
    Become an ex-smoker.

    (The Self-management psychology series) (A
Spectrum Book)
    Includes bibliographies and index.
    1. Tobacco habit.   I. Lichtenstein, Edward, joint
author.   II. Title.
RC567.D36   616.8'65'0651   78-1679
ISBN 0-13-072249-9
ISBN 0-13-072231-6 pbk.

A SPECTRUM BOOK

10   9   8   7   6   5   4   3   2   1

Printed in the United States of America

PRENTICE-HALL INTERNATIONAL, INC., *London*
PRENTICE-HALL OF AUSTRALIA PTY. LIMITED, *Sydney*
PRENTICE-HALL OF CANADA, LTD., *Toronto*
PRENTICE-HALL OF INDIA PRIVATE LIMITED, *New Delhi*
PRENTICE-HALL OF JAPAN, INC., *Tokyo*
PRENTICE-HALL OF SOUTHEAST ASIA PTE. LTD., *Singapore*
WHITEHALL BOOKS LIMITED, *Wellington, New Zealand*

Contents

chapter 2
Finding Out about Your Personal Smoking Habit   14

chapter 3
Deep Muscular Relaxation   26

section II
Calling It Quits (weeks 2 and 3)   39

chapter 4
Nonaversive Methods: Choices 1 and 2   43

chapter 5
Aversive Smoking: Choice 3   51

section III
Remaining an Ex-Smoker
(week 4 and beyond) 67

chapter 6
Changing The Smoking Signals 71

chapter 7
Managing Your Thoughts 83

chapter 8
Benefits of Not Smoking 97

chapter 9
Successful Weight Management 107

Preface

Is this book for you? This book has been written for the person who wants to learn how to become a permanent ex-smoker. *We view smoking as a learned behavior.* Unlike eating and drinking, smoking is not a natural activity. You learned to smoke cigarettes, and now you have to find out how to unlearn the smoking habit and substitute new ways of behaving. Most smoking programs aim only at helping people stop smoking. This program has been designed so that it also helps you *cope with and eliminate the lingering smoking urges* that would cause you to resume the habit.

Notice that we have used the word "help" several times in our description of the program found in this book. It is important for you to know that there is no magic wand or secret potion that can quickly make you stop smoking without effort. We outline a set of helpful skills that, when combined with old-fashioned personal effort, increase your chances of becoming an ex-smoker.

In keeping with this theme, this book has been written as a self-help workbook. It can also be used as the basis of individual or group treatment programs. We have provided spaces for you to write in your personal responses, and we have presented a particular sequence of activities for you to follow. You should read *actively* by *writing* in this workbook and by *doing* the tasks suggested. (Don't worry about writing in this book; it's important to do so.) The specific strategies should be used in the order in which they have been presented. Each chapter concludes with a *checklist*, where you can check off each accomplishment to see if you have met all the requirements and accomplished your goals before you go on to the next chapter. This workbook should be kept as a reference source, to be consulted when problems arise about smoking.

Nonsmoking skills have been selected because they can help you stop smoking and stay stopped. You will learn deep muscular relaxation as a substitute for smoking, ways you can change small parts of your everyday routine so that smoking urges are reduced and eventually eliminated, and ways your thinking can either support or undermine your efforts to become an ex-smoker.

The book is divided into two major parts: skills for becoming an ex-smoker (Sections I–IV) and a Resource Appendix on smoking issues (Section V). In the first part, smoking-control skills are presented in three stages: (1) preparing to quit, (2) quitting, and (3) remaining an ex-smoker over time. The Resource Appendix presents a more detailed look at common questions asked during smoking treatment. For example, what about hypnosis? Is weight gain an automatic consequence of quitting smoking? What is the research evidence for behavioral approaches to the modification of smoking behavior? The emerging trends in smoking control are presented so that they may help you see the "big picture" of your personal effort to quit, including, for example, occupational approaches to smoking control and primary prevention in schools. The reviews include reference citations that allow the serious reader and the professional reader to pursue interesting topics in even greater detail.

We have not included a lot of facts and figures on the dangers of continued smoking. We feel that most smokers—especially those who pick up this book—have already made a personal decision based on the important reasons for quitting. In addition, the dangers, even if recognized, do not tell you *how* to manage your life so that you can actually stop smoking! Many smokers, perhaps as many as 90 percent, would like to stop smoking, but they are not sure of their skills—or their motivation—for reaching that goal. Labels such as "willpower" are often used to explain some mysterious, intangible ingredient or trait that successful people seem to have but unsuccessful people apparently lack. By using the procedures described in this program, with careful attention and consistent effort, you can create the so-called willpower needed to increase your chances of becoming a permanent ex-smoker.

A final word before you embark upon becoming an ex-smoker: we believe that everyone who uses the program described in this book has a good chance of success. However, persons in the midst of major personal problems or crises (divorce, death of loved ones, job problems) may not have the time or concentration for this effort. Effort and hard work are probably the most important ingredients in your personal success.

Many people collaborated with us on smoking-research projects that produced several of the methods described in this book. Drs. Stephen Kopel and Russell Glasgow played a particularly important part in developing the self-administered format of the program. We would also like to recognize the following persons for their invaluable help in preparing this book: Carl Thoresen, Lynne Lumsden, Kathy Danaher, Patti Mathis, and Jane Ganter-Neary. A number of organizations generously supplied reports, information, and assistance, including the American Cancer Society, the National Cancer Institute, the National Interagency Council on Smoking and Health, and the Center for Disease Control. The Stanford Heart Disease Prevention Program, Stanford University School of Medicine, and the Department of Psychology at the University of Oregon provided supportive environments for our writing.

section I

Preparing to Become an Ex-Smoker (week 1)

In picking up this book, you have already indicated that you want some direction and guidance to increase your chances of becoming an ex-smoker. The directions we offer may sometimes seem to be asking too much of your time or energy; that's understandable. But you should remind yourself that the pace and structure for this program have been carefully determined. So use the strategies according to the order and timing outlined in the book.

These points are discussed now because you will be asked to spend at least one week in preparing to quit before you actually try to stop smoking! Patience will be needed as you begin to keep track of your personal pattern of smoking and start learning relaxation skills that will be critical to your later success.

The first week of work will involve learning two new skills—keeping a smoking diary and learning deep muscular relaxation. At the same time, you will learn about the psychology of your smoking habit.

The skills you use in preparing not to smoke will set the stage for the more detailed and somewhat more technical activities in later sections. Since this is your first step in learning not to smoke, start out on the right foot by making sure you do a fine job of it. Success in the beginning can really help you later on.

chapter 1

The Psychology of Cigarette Smoking

Have you ever asked yourself why so many people continue smoking despite what they know about its costs and its dangers? More and more people acknowledge the dangers and risks of their smoking, yet this awareness has not translated into permanent behavior change. A recent survey indicated that 60 percent of current adult smokers have made at least one serious attempt to try to break the smoking habit. You, too, may have already personally discovered the fact that smoking is a tenacious habit that can be extremely difficult to stop. Maybe you have even felt that it is impossible to change—"What's the use in trying?"

   This beginning chapter presents some information about the cigarette habit that may help to explain its strength and the difficulty in trying to stop. Different factors are involved in starting to smoke, continuing, and trying to stop. Each of these critical points will be discussed separately.

As you read this section you should consider your own personal smoking history. The better your understanding of your own habit, the more prepared you will be to become an ex-smoker. Of course, increased understanding and awareness is almost never enough to help you to stop smoking, but it will set the stage for the skills you will learn in later sections of the book.

STARTING TO SMOKE:
THE BEGINNING OF THE HABIT

A number of important research reports have revealed the factors that encourage the adoption of the smoking habit. Most smokers begin smoking relatively early in life, usually well before they reach the age of 20. Recent statistics suggest a growing trend toward early adoption. Psychosocial influences are responsible for this early experimentation. Young people begin puffing on cigarettes because of curiosity, rebellion, pressures to conform with smoking peers, and the hope of appearing more grown-up and sophisticated. Many of these motives involve the self-image of young smokers or the way others see them (see Figure 1).

While the evidence is not so clear about the factors involved in adopting the habit later in life, clinical experience suggests it may occur at times of stress or unusual disruption in the daily routine, such as death in the family, divorce, moving to a new community, or change of jobs.

The novice smoker must *learn how to smoke* since the initial experiences of inhaling tobacco smoke are usually quite unpleasant—even nauseating. With practice, the person

Figure 1
Factors in Starting and Stopping Cigarette Smoking

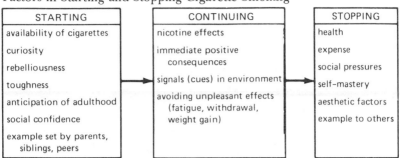

STARTING	CONTINUING	STOPPING
availability of cigarettes	nicotine effects	health
curiosity	immediate positive consequences	expense
rebelliousness		social pressures
toughness	signals (cues) in environment	self-mastery
anticipation of adulthood	avoiding unpleasant effects (fatigue, withdrawal, weight gain)	aesthetic factors
social confidence		example to others
example set by parents, siblings, peers		

Adapted from M. A. H. Russell, The smoking habit and its classification. *The Practitioner*, 1974, *212*, 719–800.

learns how to adjust the tempo of puffing and the depth of inhalation so that a tolerable mixture of outside (sidestream) air and tobacco smoke is drawn into the lungs. Once learned in this manner, the smoking habit assumes a more pronounced chemical motivation through the effects of nicotine.

CONTINUING
THE SMOKING HABIT

Nicotine is a very potent alkaloid that acts as a deadly poison in sufficient concentration. Did you know that nicotine is used as an insecticide? In normal smoking, however, the concentration of nicotine does not reach acute toxic levels. In addition to being poisonous, nicotine has been found to act as a powerful reward in man and animals. In other words, it is not necessary to learn to like the effects of nicotine since it is a natural "hooker"; the attractiveness is wired into our physical system. Smokers provide themselves with a separate

5

dose of nicotine every time they take a puff on a cigarette; thus there is a multitude of separate doses being transmitted rapidly to the brain. And the nicotine reward reaches the brain very quickly—in about 7 1/2 seconds after inhaling.

Smokers appear to develop a personally "satisfying level of nicotine" from the daily smoking routine. Reductions in the nicotine content of cigarettes are usually compensated for by inhaling deeper and/or by smoking more cigarettes per day. Consider the number of cigarettes you consume per year (even 1 pack per day = 7,224 cigarettes per year!) and the fact that there are approximately eight separate doses (puffs) of nicotine from *each* cigarette (see Table 1).

Table 1
Cumulative Smoking Statistics

Daily Count		*Monthly Count*		*Yearly Count*	
cigarettes	*puffs*	*cigarettes*	*puffs*	*cigarettes*	*puffs*
10	80	301	2,408	3,612	28,896
15	120	452	3,612	5,424	43,344
20	160	602	4,816	7,224	57,792
25	200	752	6,020	9,024	72,240
30	240	903	7,224	10,836	86,688
35	280	1,054	8,428	12,648	101,136
40	320	1,204	9,632	14,448	115,584
45	360	1,354	10,836	16,248	130,032

For all of its documented powerful effects on the body, nicotine alone does not explain why it is so difficult for many smokers to break the habit. It is here that psychosocial factors play a key role.

The purely *psychological* aspects of smoking contribute to its strength. The sheer repetition of the habit establishes it as a major part of your normal routine. Because it is possible to smoke in so many situations while involved with different activities, the smoking habit becomes strongly associated with almost every part of your daily routine. (It is hard to smoke in the shower, but some have tried!) Think for a moment about the wide range of actions associated with smoking a cigarette. Have you ever carefully observed smokers going through their smoking routine? It is not just pipe smokers who perform elaborate rituals! In effect, the habit becomes strongly linked to other parts of your behavior. Your hands, fingers, mouth, and breathing, as they are used in lighting, puffing on, and extinguishing cigarettes, become tied to other aspects of your behavior.

If these associated activities are pleasurable, then such positive experiences carry over to make your smoking more pleasurable. This may be the reason that cigarettes after work or a satisfying meal seem particularly enjoyable. You are pairing a pleasurable event—the good feelings after a satisfying meal or accomplishment at finishing your work—with a cigarette. Smoking can also provide a convenient way to escape from the unpleasant feelings of tension, anxiety, embarrassment, boredom, and fatigue. It is something to do, something that can get you away from unpleasant or dissatisfying experiences. And because it does, smoking is strengthened. (Any behavior which helps us to avoid or escape from unpleasant circumstances is strengthened. This law of learning is called by the technical term negative reinforcement.)

Learning of this type makes it possible for the same smoker to reach for a cigarette while relaxing and having a good time, while bored and filling up time, while tense and upset, and while tired and in need of a lift. No other substance provides so many kinds of reinforcement, is so readily and cheaply available, and can be used in so many different settings. It is not surprising that cigarette advertising stresses these features of smoking.

Many smokers continue smoking and have trouble stopping because they fear the unpleasant consequences of quitting. The so-called withdrawal symptoms often described in overdramatic terms ("climbing a wall," "going to pieces," "going crazy") help to dissuade many individuals. Most of you have had the experience of wanting a cigarette but not being able to smoke, perhaps because you were in a situation where smoking was prohibited. Your craving became stronger and your discomfort increased until you were able to terminate both craving and discomfort with a smoke. Such experiences pair cigarettes with relief from discomfort and greatly strengthen the smoking habit (another example of negative reinforcement).

Many smokers report that they continue the habit because they fear a rapid gain in weight if they do not smoke. (We discuss the weight control problem as it relates to smoking in Chapter 9 and in Part A of the Resource Appendix.)

Think about your own smoking habit and list your personal reasons for smoking in the spaces below. For example, one smoker listed avoiding weight gain, coping with tension, and keeping hands busy.

Personal Reasons for Smoking

1. _____

2. _____

3. _____

4. _____

5. _____

6. _____

STOPPING THE SMOKING HABIT

There are, however, many powerful reasons to stop smoking. These tend to be personal. The broad categories typically include impaired health, expense, social pressures to quit, the desire to manage personal behavior, and the desire to set a good example for others. Consider your reasons for wanting to quit at this time, and fill in the spaces below so you can make a permanent list. Think about your reasons carefully and try to state them in specific, personal terms. Do not merely write "health": specify the particular health risk that concerns you and/or specify the improvement in your health that will occur when you stop smoking.

For example, you may write "worried about getting emphysema like my brother-in-law" or "won't find myself gasping for breath after climbing a flight of stairs." Include specific personal reasons for both the risk of smoking and the benefits of stopping.

Personal Reasons for Quitting

1. —————————————————————————————

2. —————————————————————————————

3. —————————————————————————————

4. —————————————————————————————

5. —————————————————————————————

6. —————————————————————————————

7. —————————————————————————————

8. ——————————————————————————————

9. ——————————————————————————————

10. —————————————————————————————

BEHAVIORAL MODEL FOR SMOKING

Many people view smoking as a sympton of some inner need or problem that must be resolved before quitting can be accomplished. You may have found some personal motives for your smoking by considering the factors that may have led you to start and then continue smoking. But, as was outlined in Table 1, there are different motives in starting, continuing, and stopping the smoking habit.

It is important to think about smoking as a learned behavior or complex habit that is maintained by conditions in your everyday environment, that is, the situations and circumstances of what you do at home, at work, and in other settings. To successfully break the habit, you will have to do some redesigning, some rearranging of your personal environment. "Environment" describes situations and settings, such as the actions of another person or the effect of a particular room, as well as cognitive or mental events, such as certain feelings and thoughts you have.

Smoking can be considered as a chain with three links: *Signals–Behavior–Consequences.* Signals are the environmental events that seem to compel you to smoke. The behavior, of course, is actually smoking. The consequences are those effects that smoking has on both you and others. The consequences of smoking can be positive—feelings of pleasure, reduction of tension—or negative—feelings of guilt for having smoked, a fiery throat, painful coughing. It helps to distinguish between immediate or short-term consequences and long-term consequences for your health. The more enjoyable, attractive aspects of smoking are the more immediate results, and thus they often *outweigh* the long-term dangerous effects.

As a general rule, learning occurs when behaviors yield immediate, positive consequences; behaviors tend not to be repeated when they produce negative consequences. You can apply the behavioral framework to almost any smoking episode in your personal smoking pattern. Consider the following example:

> You are at a party and see friends who are smoking. Experiencing an urge for a cigarette, you light up and smoke. You enjoy the cigarette and perhaps feel a little more relaxed.

Seeing friends smoke is an external signal for smoking that causes you to experience a smoking urge. The lighting up of the cigarette is the behavior itself, while the enjoyment and feeling of relaxation is the positive consequence. Looking at smoking in this way allows you to consider three major targets for changing the smoking habit: (a) the signals (antecedent cues), which precede smoking, can be modified; (b) the experience of smoking urges can be attacked; and (c) the consequences of smoking can be changed (see Figure 2).

PROBLEM-SOLVING PERSPECTIVE

Once you start to learn about the possible influences on your smoking habit, you can begin to introduce various changes in the normal routine so that (a) your smoking can be elimi-

Figure 2

Targets for Modifying Your Smoking Habit

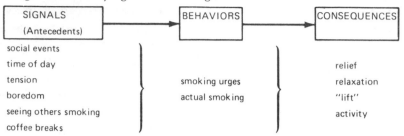

Of course, the eventual long-term consequences of chronic smoking include cardiovascular disease, lung cancer, and chronic obstructive lung disease as well.

nated, (b) your experience of smoking urges can be eliminated, and (c) nonsmoking substitute behaviors can be learned and continually practiced.

At the beginning of this program, you will be using procedures to help you stop smoking. For the most part, these proceed in a step-by-step fashion. Later, when you attack your smoking urges, you will have to become much more creative and make decisions about how and when situations or thoughts are influencing your smoking urges—and then take action to change the routine. You will learn to become an effective problem-solver, a person who can rely on personal skills to understand smoking behavior and make effective changes that allow you to manage your own life.

SUMMARY

Different factors and incentives influence starting, continuing, and stopping smoking. Smoking is a difficult habit to break because of the rewarding effects of nicotine and the

12

psychological strength of the habit. The behavioral approach to smoking control considers signals, behaviors, and consequences. All of these must be changed for you to become an ex-smoker.

Checklist

———— List your personal reasons for smoking.

———— List your personal reasons for wanting to stop smoking.

———— Be familiar with the behavioral model of smoking behavior.

———— Understand the problem-solving perspective of being an ex-smoker.

chapter 2

Finding Out about Your Personal Smoking Habit

Everyone who smokes knows something about his or her personal smoking pattern. It may seem perfectly obvious that you smoke more during particular events or at certain times of the day. Perhaps you even know the number of cigarettes you smoke each day. All of these bits of information are useful as you try to come to grips with your personal smoking habit, but they do not really provide for a successful cessation program.

You need to know exactly how much you smoke daily, the number of smoking urges you feel daily, the intensity of your smoking urges, the timing of urges and actual smoking, and the situations that are associated with your smoking. This may seem like a lot of information—and it is. Fortunately, there is an easy method for recording this data in a convenient smoking diary.

14

THE SMOKING DIARY

To gather information, you should carry a small (3″ × 5″) notebook with you for at least the next five weeks to record information. A sample page is presented in Figure 3. Make copies of this page so that you have a total of at least 13 pages in your smoking diary. Alternatively, you can rule off your own pages on 3 × 5 index cards.

Notice that the diary page contains enough room to cover three days. Each day is broken up into hours (A.M. and P.M.) so that you can record the time you smoked each cigarette as well as when you experienced each smoking urge. One helpful way to remember to record your smoking is to attach the record notebook or cards to your cigarette pack—perhaps with a rubber band.

Smoking Urges

Start by paying attention to the experiences that occur prior to having a cigarette. This feeling is defined here as a smoking urge. The system for noting your urges is presented below. You will use an urge rating scale with five levels of intensity.

Urge Rating Scale: "I want a cigarette . . ."

1. a little ("not really at all").
2. somewhat ("perhaps").
3. a moderate amount ("vague desire").
4. much ("need").
5. very much ("craving").

Once you experience an urge to smoke, you should pick a number from the rating scale that best describes how much

Figure 3
Format of Your Smoking Diary

		DAY		DAY		DAY	
		AM	PM	AM	PM	AM	PM
		Tot. =		Tot. =		Tot. =	
	12						
	1						
	2						
	3						
	4						
	5						
	6						
	7						
	8						
	9						
	10						
	11						

FRONT

KEY SITUATIONS

Day _____ :

Day _____ :

Day _____ :

BACK

The front of the data page provides space for recording smoking urges and the back, for key situations that signal these urges.

you want that cigarette. Then write the number into the diary on the appropriate page and in the appropriate time slot. Different people evaluate their smoking urges in somewhat different ways. Your task is to be as consistent with your own personal ratings as possible.

Cigarettes Smoked

The smoking urges that lead to your having a cigarette should be indicated, too. All you need to do is draw a circle around the urge rating you selected according to the rules just mentioned. At the end of the day, add up all of the cigarettes you smoked that day and write this total in the top section of the data page. Draw a circle around it as well.

Sleeping. It is helpful to pick out the patterns of your activities as they relate to your smoking. Cross out those hours during which you sleep.

Situations. You may have noticed that the front of the data page includes no room for describing the situations that are linked to your smoking pattern. By "situations," we mean any activities, events, or feelings that consistently seem to signal your smoking. You should think about which situations stand out and then describe them briefly on the back side of the data page (as shown in Figure 3). Do this at least three times each day. Information about the links between situations and your smoking will be important in the strategies that will be presented later.

An Example of the Smoking Diary

To help put the entire data collection procedure together for you, refer to Figure 4 and to the example that follows.

Figure 4
Example of a Filled-in Page from a Smoking Diary

		DAY 1		DAY 2		DAY 3	
		AM	PM	AM	PM	AM	PM
		Tot. =	②	Tot. =	⑲	Tot. =	
	12			④③			
	1			③ 2 1			
	2		④				
	3			③③③			
	4						
	5		3	4			
	6		②	④② 1			
	7			⑤			
	8			⑤③②			
	9			2 ④④			
	10			⑤⑤	⑤		
	11			③①			

FRONT

KEY SITUATIONS

Day __1__ : with wine after lunch
with coffee after dinner

Day __2__ : while getting up in the morning – _hurry_
during breakfast
driving to work & back home at night
business meeting @ mid afternoon (_pressure_)
tired late at night

Day __3__ :

BACK

Example: Suppose you have an urge to smoke at 2:10 P.M. and you rate it as a #4. You immediately take out your smoking diary and write the number 4 in the 2 P.M. time box for the appropriate day (see Day 1, Figure 4). Let us assume further that you go ahead and smoke a cigarette as a result of that urge; then you simply circle the number four (④). At 5 P.M. you experience a #3 urge but you choose not to smoke because it occurs during dinner. At 6:30, however, you have a #2 urge, so you go ahead and smoke at that time. All these data are presented in the example page (Figure 4). Be sure that you fully understand how to keep track of your data in this manner. Note that Day 2 on the sample page is more completely filled out. It is possible for you to record the data for many urges and cigarettes in the spaces provided. At the end of each day, circle the total number of cigarettes smoked in the space at the top of the A.M. and P.M. columns. Also cross out those times when you were asleep. Be sure to list the important situations on the back. *Note:* Make sure that you rate all the urges that precede each of the cigarettes you smoke. This is true even though you may feel that some of your smoking is so automatic that it seems almost unconscious. Force yourself to pay attention to the smoking urges so that you become more aware of your smoking habit.

Summary

You will immediately begin to keep track of your normal smoking for at least the next week. Do NOT try to stop smoking at this time. The smoking diary should be kept with you at all times so that you can indicate the cigarettes you smoke, the preceding urges, and the times and settings of your smoking. The data pages should contain the following:

1. numbers from 1 through 5, indicating your evaluation of the smoking urges you experience.

2. circled numbers indicating the smoking urges that were followed by lighting up and smoking a cigarette.

3. comments or situations in which you smoked (back of page).

GETTING SYSTEMATIC: KEEPING A SMOKING GRAPH

Once you begin to use your smoking diary you will need to have a way of organizing the information you collect. The best arrangement involves keeping track of your cigarettes and smoking urges on the graph presented in Figure 5. You will be able to see your progress quickly and clearly by glancing at this graph. This visual "feedback" from your graph will help reward your efforts. Post a copy of the graph in a convenient place for recording and review, on the refrigerator or near a mirror, for example.

Graphing your personal data requires an introduction to some fundamentals. First, there are two straight lines in the graph that intersect at the lower lefthand corner. The vertical axis represents the number of units (in either cigarettes or urges) that you experience. The horizontal axis represents the time span of your program and is marked off in days using the numbers 1 through 30.

In making a graph, you first record the number of smoking and smoking-urge events you experience each day. Cigarettes are indicated by dots while smoking urges are indicated by small x's. Then connect the dots and connect the x's so that you have two lines moving from left to right across the middle of the graph (see the example in Figure 6).

Figure 5
Your Personal Smoking Graph

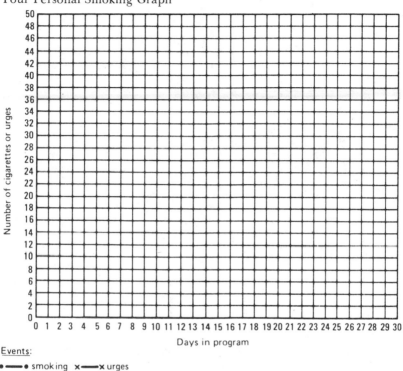

Events:

●———● smoking   x———x urges

At first, you should expect that the lines will overlap, because it is quite common for smokers who continue with normal smoking to obey each smoking urge by smoking a cigarette. Later, when you make a strong effort to quit smoking, you will probably find that the urges actually increase while the cigarettes smoked drop toward zero.

You will notice that the lines wiggle a bit from day to day. This points out graphically those daily variations in your smoking habit. Your rate of smoking at first may seem lower than you remember. This is a common experience for many people because rough estimates of daily smoking tend to be a

21

Figure 6

A Sample Smoking Graph

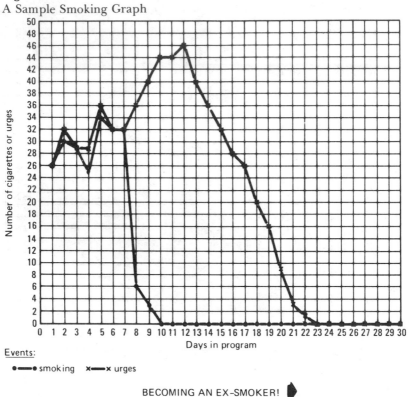

Events:

●━━● smoking   ✕━━✕ urges

BECOMING AN EX-SMOKER! ▶

little high. Also the very act of keeping track of smoking in the smoking diary may somewhat influence your normal smoking pattern. Sometimes persons tend to reduce their smoking so that they will not have to record it. Unfortunately, the helpful effects of carefully observing and graphing your urges and smoking experiences usually are not enough to stop you from smoking permanently.

PINPOINTING SIGNALS
IN YOUR DAILY PATTERN

Once you have begun keeping track of your smoking, you will undoubtedly identify certain consistencies or patterns in your personal habit. Is there something about the time of day that prompts your smoking? Is eating an activity that accompanies much of your smoking? Look at the timing of your smoking, the intensity of urges, and the situations that you may have scribbled on the back of the data page for information about the patterns of your smoking.

Link your smoking urges—how much you want or need a cigarette—to specific signal situations. Table 2 shows how this can be done from the information in your smoking diary. A number of common signal situations are listed. Decide how your urges relate to signal situations and then add the signals from your diary. Use the *Urge Rating Scale* you used for your smoking diary (under "Smoking Urges"):

1	2	3	4	5
A little	Somewhat	A moderate amount	Much	Very much

In determining how strong your urges for a cigarette are, count *Light Urges* as mostly 1 and 2 urge ratings, *Moderate Urges* as mostly 3 and some 4 urge ratings, and *Strong Urges* as mostly 5 and some 4 urge ratings.

Table 2
Common Smoking Signal Situations

How strong are your urges for a cigarette?

Situations	Light Urges	Moderate Urges	Strong Urges
after a meal			
while drinking coffee			
while drinking an alcoholic beverage			
after finishing a job			
while on the phone			
while reading or studying			
while watching TV			
while tense or anxious			
during an argument			

Continue to keep track of your smoking and your smoking urges, because this information will be important in planning the most effective and long-lasting treatment for your habit. Keeping records may prove to be a bother—but it is important for you to interrupt your highly practiced smoking habit and become much more aware of it. Control strategies described later in the book will be based on some of the key information you will begin recording from now on. Be thorough and accurate with your smoking diary and smoking graph. Above all, don't deceive yourself or become "forgetful" about recording your urges and smoking. Learning to solve the problems of becoming a permanent ex-smoker requires accurate and reliable information.

SUMMARY

The first step in becoming an ex-smoker involves keeping a record of your personal smoking habit. Records can be accurately kept in a small booklet—the smoking diary—that you will have to make and then carry with you for the remainder of the program. A method was described for noting smoking urges (and their intensity), cigarettes smoked, and important daily events on the back of the page. The smoking data can then be charted on your personal smoking graph. Finally, patterns in your smoking should be identified and listed on the chart provided.

Checklist

——— Make your smoking diary by copying the page in the book.

——— Carry your smoking diary with you at all times, recording smoking episodes, urges, and events.

——— Understand the concept of smoking signals.

——— List some of the patterns you see in your personal smoking habit.

——— Record the smoking data from your smoking diary on your personal smoking graph.

chapter 3

Deep Muscular Relaxation

In one way or another all of us learn how to handle the stresses of everyday living. Some of our daily pressures can be traced to external sources. For example, consider the pressure you feel when you push to meet a pressing deadline at work or when you have to hurry around the house to get ready for visiting relatives. At other times, the pressures seem to be more self-inflicted, in that they involve behaviors we impose on ourselves. Excessive worrying about how we look or how we perform on a test are good examples of internal sources of common tensions.

Experiencing stress is a common situation in our society and we have had to learn by trial and error how to lessen the upsetting effects of daily tension. During the 1970's, there has been a tremendous explosion of interest in specific strategies to help persons reduce tension. Some are familiar: yoga, meditation, and self-hypnosis. All these popular programs offer some relief to certain persons. But we have decided to describe a well-researched approach to relaxation that can be learned through a step-by-step strategy. We will outline these steps in this chapter. Even if you have learned how to relax using other methods, you can still benefit by learning the procedure described in this chapter, called *deep muscular relaxation*, or simply DMR.

DMR PROCEDURE

This method has been used successfully in clinical settings for many years to help persons relieve tension, reduce fears, and eliminate varied problems—excessive fears of heights, water, flying, snakes, driving, public speaking, social relations, and many similar problems. It has also helped people cope with stressful work situations, medical and dental treatments, and other necessary but nonetheless trying experiences.

In DMR, you learn ways to identify the muscles that grow tense when you feel pressures and, once this identification has been made, reduce that tension effectively and efficiently right on the spot. The program does not include the use of any medications (sedatives) nor does it require you to adopt any religious or philosophical beliefs. But it does require some effort. You will practice a set of exercises that enables you to identify and then reduce your levels of bodily tension.

We have included relaxation in this book because it offers an effective, research-proven tool that can help eliminate your need for cigarettes to reduce tension. Relaxation can also act as a replacement for your smoking habit and can help soften so-called withdrawal reactions of anxiety and irritability. First you need to learn and practice how to relax. Concentrate on learning the procedures described in the remainder of this chapter.

DMR EXERCISES

As in learning any complex skill, the first steps may seem awkward and frustrating. Once you progress beyond the initial stages, however, you will be able to quickly and efficiently relax on command—wherever and whenever necessary. At this point, you may experience the satisfaction of starting to increase your ability to manage your own reactions and take an important step toward becoming an ex-smoker.

Tension-Reduction Practice

The first part of learning DMR calls for you to set aside time for intensive practice. Early practice sessions will take 35 to 45 minutes and will require a room where you will not be disturbed by family members, friends, or pets. The room should have a comfortable chair (a recliner is especially good!) or a bed that allows you to assume a reclining position with your hands at your sides. Or you may lie on a carpeted floor. Once the room arrangements have been made and you have set aside adequate time for practicing DMR, you should follow these steps:

1. Loosen tight clothing, remove glasses and shoes.

2. Assume a comfortable, reclining position and close your eyes.

3. Focus all of your attention on specific sets of muscles.

4. Tense and study the tension in the specific muscle sets for 10 to 15 seconds, and then relax the same muscles, noticing the difference between tension and relaxation.

5. Review all muscles, use tension-relaxation where necessary while taking slow breaths.

There are four major groups of muscles: in the hands and arms; the head, face, and neck; upper torso; and the legs and feet. Each group contains several sets of muscles. The sets and the order in which they should be relaxed are shown in Table 3. As a rule, you should begin with the muscle sets outlined below, and then feel free to add and subtract muscles as you begin to identify the location of your personal pockets of bodily tension.

Table 3
Deep Muscular Relaxation:
Muscle Groups and Sets

Hands and Arms	*Upper Torso*
1. hands (r & l)	8. upper back
2. upper arms (r & l biceps)	9. lower back
3. shoulders (r & l)	10. stomach
Head, Face, and Neck	*Legs and Feet*
4. neck	11. thighs (r & l)
5. forehead	12. calves (r & l)
6. face	
7. throat & tongue	

You should be aware of possible problems you may have in using the DMR procedure. Trying too hard and expecting dramatic, immediate relief can actually prevent successful relaxation. Most people need practice to learn relaxation. Distractions (noises, interruptions, unwanted thoughts) can also disrupt effective practice. Pick a quiet room and concentrate on a pleasant thought. Unpleasant sensations such as cramps or dizziness may occur, but these can usually be avoided. Finally, feeling sleepy is a good sign because it shows that you are getting relaxed. But falling asleep at this time should be avoided, because you need to be wide awake to practice the entire DMR procedure.

We have listed the basic steps and the specific muscle sets that you will work on in DMR practice sessions in your home. To give you an even better flavor for how the home-practice session should go, we are including a transcript of an actual relaxation session conducted by one of the authors, as follows:

Make a fist with your right hand. Make the fist tighter and tighter, and hold it as you study the tension in the fingers, knuckles, and forearm. Now let it go and notice the tingling sensation as the relaxation spreads through these muscles. Repeat that now; tighten your right fist and notice how tight all of the muscles become as you hold your fist closed. Hold it tighter and tighter, and now let it go. Let all of those muscles relax.

Now do the same exercise with the left hand. Make a fist and study the tension in the fingers, knuckles, and the forearm. Hold that fist as tightly as possible, and now let it completely relax. Feel the tension dissolve away, to be replaced by the warm, pleasant sensations of relaxation. Repeat that exercise now. Make a fist with that left hand and hold it tighter and tighter. And then let it go and note the difference between the tension and the relaxation in those muscles.

Concentrate on your upper arms now. Bend your right arm at the elbow so that you bring your hand toward your shoulder. Make a muscle—a Popeye-like bicep muscle—and hold it as tight as you can while you focus all your attention on the feelings of tension. Notice the pull beneath your elbow and the tightness of the right side of your chest and right shoulder. Hold it now, and now relax. Let all of the tension leave those muscles, and allow your arm to rest again comfortably by your side. Repeat that again now. Make a muscle with your right arm by bringing the hand toward the shoulder. Notice the tension in the muscles of the arm, shoulder, and chest. Move your hand around while keeping the bicep tight, and study the small changes in levels of tension. Hold it tight, and now let it go. Let the muscles of the arm smooth out and relax again.

Repeat the same procedure now with your left arm. Bend it at the elbow and make a muscle. For many people, these muscles won't be as well developed as those in the right arm. But do your best by making a Popeye-like muscle with your left arm. Study the tension as you hold it tight, and now let your left arm relax. Let all of the tension go, and study the pleasant, warm sensation of relaxation returning to those muscles. Repeat the procedure again. Make a muscle with your left arm and study the tension. Move your hand around a bit, and notice the small changes in tension in various muscles. Hold it tighter and tighter, as if you are holding up a great weight, and now let the arm relax. Throw away all of the tension in those muscles, and study the difference between relaxation and tension.

Now lift the tips of your shoulders in an exaggerated shrug so that they almost touch your ears. Lift them up now, and study the tension in the shoulders, neck, and chest muscles. Hold those muscles as tight as you can, thinking that you are a puppet and your entire weight is suspended by your shoulders, and now let all those muscles go. Just let the tension go, and allow yourself to experience the pleasant sensations of relaxation. Now return to those muscles. Tighten your shoulder muscles by lifting your shoulders almost up to your ears in an exaggerated shrug. Hold those muscles as tight as you can now—tighter and tighter. Now let them relax. Just let all these muscles lose their tension. You should begin to feel comfortably relaxed now, especially in the muscles covered so far.

Continue on to the muscles in your head and throat now. Wrinkle your forehead by lifting your eyebrows to the top of your head. Just lift the eyebrows and study the tension in the muscles of your forehead. These muscles signal tension for many people, so it's important for you to learn the subtle levels of tension now. Hold those tighter and tighter, and now let all of the muscles go. Just let them completely relax and notice the tingling sensations as relaxation spreads through and smooths these areas. Try that exercise again. Lift your eyebrows up so that deep wrinkles appear in your forehead. Hold them there now while you study the tension. And now let the tension go. Notice the difference between relaxation and tension.

Now wrinkle your nose and make an exaggerated smile. It may help if you imagine yourself smelling a lemon and suddenly recoiling from the pungent aroma. Hold all those muscles tight now, and study the tension in these muscles. Now let them all go and allow your face to resume a more comfortable position.

Now try pushing your tongue into the roof of your mouth and feel the muscles of your throat and mouth become more and more tense. Notice the tension in your throat as you push your tongue into the roof of the mouth. Hold it there, and now let it relax. Allow all the muscles to relax and your tongue to drift back down to assume a comfortable position in your mouth.

Now you can concentrate on the muscles in your neck. Try pushing your head back into the pillow or chair so that the muscles of your neck grow tight. Push back and study the tension in your neck and shoulders. Hold it there, and now let it all go. Just throw away the tension, and notice the difference between relaxation and tension. Try repeating that exercise with your neck. Push back hard into the pillow or chair until the muscles grow very tight. Hold it there while you pay attention to the tension. Hold it, and now let it go. Just let the muscles of your neck relax. You might want to slowly move your head around a bit to really loosen up these muscles.

Now you can arch your back by trying to touch your shoulders behind you. Lift your back, and study the tension in the muscles from your shoulders down to your lower back. Hold it, and now let it all go—just let those muscles relax as you sink deeply back into a comfortable position. Try arching your back again and tighten up all of the muscles. Hold those muscles tight while paying attention to the tension, and now let all of those muscles relax while you return to a comfortable position.

To tighten the muscles of your chest, take a deep breath and hold it for a while. Go ahead and take a deep breath, and hold it in. Hold it, and notice the increasing tension in the muscles of your chest. Hold it, and now let it go out very slowly. Study the reduction in tension as you slowly breathe out. Now repeat that exercise again. Take a deep breath, and hold it while you notice the sensation of tension. Hold your chest muscles tight and then slowly let it all out as you notice increasing relaxation.

Now try pushing out your stomach and tightening the muscles in your abdomen. Push and push while you study the tension in these muscles. Hold them tight, and now let the tension go. Just relax those muscles now. Now, instead of pushing out, try pulling those stomach muscles in. Really tighten them up, and now let the tension go. Notice the difference between pushing out and pulling in—and, of course, the difference between the tension and the relaxation.

In tensing the muscles in your legs, try tightening the upper part of your right leg. Imagine that you are about to kick a ball 100 yards. Really feel those muscles tighten up in anticipation of kicking the ball. Study the tension, and let the tension go. Just let your leg relax now. Let's repeat that exercise. Tense your right upper leg, and hold it there for a few seconds. Hold it and hold it, and now let it all go. Just let your leg relax and sink comfortably into the chair or bed.

Make the same tension now in your left leg. Think about getting ready to kick a ball 100 yards. Feel those muscles tighten, and study that tension. All right, now let it go; let those muscles relax. Repeat this exercise one more time: Tense the muscles, pay attention to the tension, and then relax.

Finally, tighten and then relax the muscles of your lower legs and feet. To do this you should carefully rotate your feet so that your toes are pointing back towards your knee. Don't overextend these muscles because they can develop cramps. Hold the tension, and now let them relax completely. Now repeat that exercise but this time point your toes down and tighten up your calf muscles. Be careful not to tighten too much and form a cramp. Hold them tighter and tighter, and then let the muscles relax and your legs resume a comfortable position on the bed or chair.

Examine all muscles and relax those with any remaining tension—hands, upper arms, shoulders, neck, forehead (calm and smooth now), face and throat, chest, abdomen, upper and lower legs. Continue breathing slowly.

YOUR HOME DMR SESSIONS

Practice DMR by using the instructions above and the transcript of the actual relaxation practice session. You may have to read the book during the first few sessions; after some practice, however, you will become quite familiar with the DMR procedure and be able to deeply relax without any reading. You may find that you really need friends or family members to read the instructions aloud during early practice sessions. Or, you may want to use a tape recorder, which allows you to record the relaxation instructions for later use.

With the virtual explosion of interest in relaxation-skills training, additional materials that complement this text can be obtained at a reasonable cost. Audiotaped materials are particularly helpful because they supplement the DMR procedure and provide the pacing of the instructions that contribute to relaxation. Various types of relaxation tapes can be obtained from BioMonitoring Applications, Inc., 270 Madison Avenue, New York, N.Y. 10016. One of these tapes has been developed by one of the authors (B.G. Danaher, Ph.D.: *Basic Deep Muscular Relaxation in Comprehensive Smoking Cessation Program*).

More detailed instructions in relaxation that have been aimed at a general audience can be found in Gerald Rosen's book *The Relaxation Book: An Illustrated Self-Help Program* (Englewood Cliffs, N.J.: Prentice-Hall, in press). Professional consultants who wish to supervise the application of relaxation might consider Douglas Bernstein and Thomas Borkovec's *Progressive Relaxation Training: A Manual for the Helping Professions* (Champaign, Ill.: Research Press, 1973).

Practice Guide

Scheduling DMR practice sessions *in advance* often helps people follow through with the actual practice. It seems to work like a scheduled appointment. Table 4 will serve as your practice log, to help you schedule and keep track of your DMR practice sessions and evaluate your progress. Use the following rating scale to evaluate your tension before and after each session:

1	2	3	4	5	6	7	8	9	10

Not at all relaxed	Moderately relaxed	Completely, deeply relaxed

Practice Sessions 1–5

As you may have guessed, the early stages of relaxation practice guide you in the use of all your muscle sets in *non-*

Table 4
Relaxation Log

Session No.	Day/Hour	Comments	Relaxation Rating before	after
1				
2				
3				
4				
5				
6				
7				
8				
9				
10				
11				
12				

stressful situations (at home, away from interruptions and noises). Now get in a comfortable position and go through the entire DMR procedure, using the transcript as a guide. This enables your early experiences with relaxation to be both effective and enjoyable. You should do five practice sessions, going through all the sets of muscles. As you become more skilled at DMR, you will want to shorten the procedure so it can become a helpful tool in your normal routine.

Practice Sessions 6–9

The next phase of DMR practice involves becoming relaxed by identifying the *specific* muscles that are contributing to your experience of tension (not *all* your muscles). Now you should practice brief DMR while you also engage in some normal *low-stress activity* (washing the dishes, reading the newspapers, shining shoes, etc.). Thus you will learn how to use brief DMR in situations that more closely resemble your real world by relaxing only those muscles that are tense. Obviously, it is not enough for you to be able to get deeply relaxed by reclining in a soft chair and relaxing all your muscles for 35 minutes or so. You need to develop skill in becoming relaxed *quickly and privately,* pinpointing specific muscles and relaxing them quickly so that DMR can be helpful in your ordinary routine.

Practice Session 10 and Beyond

Once you have had the chance to practice brief DMR in the quiet of your own home with low-stress activities, begin to practice the skill in your working environment. Begin by selectively using DMR at coffee breaks, instead of smoking perhaps, while the stress levels are fairly low. Once this has been practiced successfully, use DMR in your ordinary routine, perhaps when stuck in traffic or when under pressure of large work loads, by (a) pinpointing tense muscles, (b) briefly tensing and relaxing, (c) telling yourself to remain calm and relaxed, and (d) breathing slowly.

You should continue using DMR in your everyday routine and become confident and assured in your new skill. Later on in this book, we will describe specific ways DMR can be used to help you become a permanent ex-smoker. Note: If you have difficulty at any stage of learning, simply back up and practice the earlier steps again.

SUMMARY

Deep muscular relaxation has been presented in a step-by-step format for easy practice. You should practice at least once a day. Practice sessions 1–5 are spent working at home on all sets of muscles, while sessions 6–9 involve the relaxation of only those specific muscles that are tense. Sessions 10 and beyond involve working on relaxation while you go through your everyday routine, using the shortened version of relaxation.

Checklist

———— Relax at least once a day following the schedule.

———— Rate your relaxation, using the relaxation log.

section II

Calling It Quits
(weeks 2 and 3)

You have now completed some beginning steps in becoming an ex-smoker. You have learned about the psychology of smoking—the factors that probably encouraged you to experiment with cigarettes, learn how to smoke competently, continue smoking over time, and, now, take an interest in stopping the habit altogether. We hope that you have practiced deep muscular relaxation so you can quickly identify those muscles that contribute to tension and that you are now able to relax those muscles effectively. You have also been keeping a smoking diary for at least a week, charting cigarettes smoked and smoking urges on a 1 to 5 point scale, and have learned how the intensity of your smoking urges is related to different situations.

The next step is to make a serious effort to stop smoking. For some people, it is not so much the stopping that seems particularly difficult. Instead, it is the ability to remain an ex-smoker, or the ability to stay stopped. Mark Twain is supposed to have stated that quitting smoking was easy, for he'd done it thousands of times! For others, however, there is a doubt and actual fear that a day cannot pass without some smoking. As some of our clients have noted, the longest period they go without cigarettes is when they are asleep. Even then, some people awake in the middle of the night to smoke and then fall asleep again!

This chapter will present several methods that have been found helpful in inducing smokers to stop—at least temporarily. We have considerable confidence that these procedures will enable you to stop smoking completely for a short period of time. Once you reach the point of being a *temporary* ex-smoker, we will turn to methods for coping with the lingering urges to smoke. It is here that you will utilize the patterns that appear in the smoking diary and adopt specific strategies that should help reduce the attraction of smoking.

We recommend that you read the section on quitting in its entirety *before* deciding which quitting method to use. You may want to try stopping on your own first and then use one of the methods described if you cannot do it. We'd like you to stop smoking by the simplest and least aversive way possible. The important thing for now is getting yourself stopped.

Making a Date to Quit

There are several methods that can help you stop smoking. A common and critically important feature to all of them is setting a *target date* for stopping. As you will learn in a later chapter, it is very easy to put off quitting the habit. By setting a specific target date for quitting, you make a personal contract that is perfectly clear. Of course, you will have to stick with the date you select—and the ways that you can reach this goal are the basic subject matter of this chapter.

We will describe three methods for quitting: (1) You can simply stop by using whatever personal method has worked for you in the past. This option is for those who have little difficulty in making at least a temporary break from smoking. (2) You can make a financial contract with yourself—or preferably with some other trusted person—so that you will lose the money deposit if you do not stop. (3) The final method involves aversive smoking, which instructs you to smoke on a schedule instead of following your normal pattern of smoking. This schedule is, of course, an unpleasant one; hence the term aversive smoking.

Choosing the Right Procedure

There are several things to consider in making the best decision on the most effective treatment for stopping:

1. You should select the first option if you find it fairly easy to stop smoking temporarily. For example, choose this option if you have stopped temporarily two or more times within the past five years.

2. You should try the second option if you have a trusted friend who will assist you in keeping track of a contract and a monetary deposit.

3. If the first two methods are not right for you, then you should use an aversive smoking procedure called *regular-paced aversive smoking* if you are more than 40 years of age, have cardiovascular or respiratory health problems, or cannot obtain physician approval for the final treatment option.

4. You can use as the final option the very unpleasant yet quite effective procedure known as *rapid smoking*.

Please read through this entire chapter first and then

make a decision after understanding the available options. Before you decide to use the rapid-smoking procedure you will have to meet the requirements and obtain the permission of your personal physician. More will be said on these points later.

Quitting Is Not Enough

One of the reasons that many people experience great difficulty in trying to stop smoking is that *they stop making much of an effort soon after they have stopped smoking.* This is understandable, yet fatal for the permanent stopping of most smokers. You are only halfway toward your goal when you stop smoking. Stopping for most people merely ushers in a period of intense effort in coping with the urges that remain. Until you cope with and eliminate most of the smoking urges that you presently have, as noted in your smoking diary, you are very likely doomed to eventual resumption. Unfortunately, the urges to smoke *increase* once you have stopped. Thus, things tend to get worse before they get better. That is why coping with urges after you have stopped smoking is the key to becoming an ex-smoker.

This chapter on quitting is presented as the first step in the work required of you to become a permanent ex-smoker. Do not throw the book aside if you stop smoking early; keep reading and working with the suggestions provided. Only in this way will you learn the skills required for being a confirmed ex-smoker.

chapter 4

Nonaversive Methods: Choices 1 and 2

This chapter describes two methods you can use to stop smoking. These methods are *nonaversive* in the sense that they do not attempt to directly increase the unpleasantness of your smoking habit. Instead, the nonaversive approaches help you mobilize your effort to stop smoking by showing you how to make contracts with yourself or a trusted friend while you aim at a specific date for quitting. Once you have stopped smoking, you should turn to Section III and begin using the various strategies designed to help you attack and overcome your remaining smoking urges.

Remember, you should read this entire section before you decide on the best quitting method to use.

CHOICE 1: STOPPING BY YOURSELF

As mentioned earlier, many people can stop smoking with little difficulty. In fact, they may have considerable experience with quitting in the past. (Remember the point made in Mark Twain's statement.) If this applies to your experience, then you should follow the rules presented below.

Rule 1. Set a specific date and time for quitting, and write this in your personal contract (see Figure 7). The time could be as early as three days from now or as far away as next week, whichever you prefer. This date and time (early in the morning or in the evening) should be listed in the target date box. Of course you should follow through with the date, once chosen, and actually stop smoking at that time.

Figure 7

My Personal Contract for Quitting

I agree to stop all smoking on _____ *at* _____.
(target date)   (target time)

I understand that it is important for me to make a strong personal effort at this

particular time so that I can become a permanent ex-smoker. I sign this contract

as an indication of my personal commitment to stop smoking on target.

_____   _____
(your signature)   (date of signing)

Rule 2. Three days before your target date, you should cut your daily smoking in half. For example, if you smoke 20 cigarettes per day, then you should reduce that total down to only 10 cigarettes daily for the three-day period. Do NOT try to gradually reduce your smoking down to zero, however, because this will actually increase the value of each remaining cigarette and make your attempt to quit extremely frustrating. This rule is based on strong clinical evidence, so we urge you not to gradually go to zero cigarettes per day.

Rule 3. When you reach your target date, you may want to throw away all of your cigarettes. Some people like to make a ceremony out of this event. If you feel that you will panic unless you have cigarettes available somewhere (even if they are in the garage, the trunk of the car, or the attic), then you should follow your own inclinations. That is particularly true if these methods have been at least temporarily helpful to you in the past.

Rule 4. Try not to make too much out of quitting. Do not magnify it out of proportion because this may make you experience more stress and other withdrawal effects. We will have more to say about withdrawal effects later.

Rule 5. Once you have reached your target date and have successfully stopped smoking, you should turn to Chapters 6 through 10 and begin working hard on the skills you will need to help you cope with lingering smoking urges. Remember to continue keeping track of smoking urges in your smoking diary throughout this time.

CHOICE 2: STOPPING WITH HELP FROM OTHERS

The second method for stopping smoking involves arranging a contract with yourself and another person, preferably a trusted friend. The contract would involve a commitment on your part to stop smoking as of a particular date and hour following three days of reduced smoking—half usual level—as was described in the previous section. In this case, however, you also build in an added incentive—the possible loss of money! The contract states that you will forfeit money from your deposit if you fail to stop smoking. But you will receive portions of the deposit back as "payment" if you become an ex-smoker (see Figure 8).

This contract arrangement can work without the help of others; you may act as your own banker for the agreement. But many people find that asking assistance of a friend helps them stick to their contract. Of course, it is important that this friend be trusted, because putting up your money and its repayment must be governed strictly by the written contract. This friend, the "banker" in your contract, should not be a smoker and should not attempt to tell you how to quit.

There are several rules for developing a contract with the help of others as a method for stopping smoking.

Rule 1. Risk an amount of money that would hurt you if it were forfeited. Five dollars would very likely be small and insignificant to you if it were lost; $50 or $100 is more significant!

Rule 2. Choose the banker with great care. He or she can be any nonsmoker you trust, who is willing to help by taking responsibility for keeping your deposit.

Rule 3. Once the contract is signed, stick to it. There should be no changes made in the target date and the monetary agreement, because changes undermine the effectiveness of this entire procedure.

Rule 4. Decide what will be done with any forfeited money with great care. The money must *not* go to your banker. Instead, it should be payable to either a favorite

Figure 8

(Your copy)

Two-party Contract for Quitting

I agree to stop smoking on _____ *at* _____. *I have*
                                   (target date)   *(target time)*

given the sum of $ _____ *to* _____ *with the understanding that he/she*
                               (banker's name)

will send the money to _____ *if I am unable to stop smoking*
                             (organization)

according to this agreement. If I am able to stop smoking completely for the first week after the target date specified above, I will at that time receive half of the deposit back. The remaining portion of the deposit will be returned after the second week of nonsmoking (two weeks from the target date).

_____   _____
          (your signature)   *(date)*

_____   _____
          (banker's signature)   *(date)*

(Banker's copy)

Two-party Contract for Quitting

I agree to stop smoking on _____ *at* _____. *I have*
                                   (target date)   *(target time)*

given the sum of $ _____ *to* _____ *with the understanding that he/she*
                               (banker's name)

will send the money to _____ *if I am unable to stop smoking*
                             (organization)

according to this agreement. If I am able to stop smoking completely for the first week after the target date specified above, I will at that time receive half of the deposit back. The remaining portion of the deposit will be returned after the second week of nonsmoking (two weeks from the target date).

_____   _____
          (your signature)   *(date)*

_____   _____
          (banker's signature)   *(date)*

charity or, even better, your least favorite organization—one you would hate to see get your good money! Write checks in advance with the name of the least favorite organization for the banker to hold, so that payment is almost automatic if you smoke. These strategies provide a powerful incentive for you to uphold the contract.

Rule 5. Use the contract presented in Figure 8. One side should be signed by you and become your copy; it remains in this book. The other copy is kept by the trusted banker as his or her copy of the contract.

Once you have reached the point where you have stopped smoking, you should immediately turn to Section III (Chapters 6 through 9) and begin working diligently on the skills that will help you resist lingering smoking urges and become a permanent ex-smoker. Remember to keep track of smoking urges in your smoking diary throughout this time.

SUMMARY

Two methods that will help you stop smoking have been suggested. Both use a target date for quitting, along with contracts. In one case, the contract, or agreement to stop smoking, is made with yourself, while the other method involves a contract with another person. Rules for the contract procedure are outlined in the chapter.

Checklist

———— Continue keeping track of smoking and urges in the smoking diary.

———— Continue practicing relaxation.

———— Read Chapter 5 before selecting a method for quitting smoking.

———— Select a nonaversive or a smoke-aversion procedure for quitting.

———— Follow rules for method selected.

chapter 5

Aversive Smoking: Choice 3

This chapter describes two procedures that you could use to help you stop smoking. Both of the procedures involve smoke aversion—smoking in a manner that becomes highly unpleasant. Tobacco smoke is a noxious pollutant, and it can act as its own aversive element. You may be asking yourself, "Well, if it is so noxious, why haven't I found it to be unpleasant before?" The likely answer is that you have learned not to notice the unpleasantness: You have been highly successful in distracting yourself from the ongoing aversiveness of your smoking habit.

If you think back over the time when you first began to experiment with smoking, you will probably recall that you felt somewhat nauseous after the first few puffs. It was only after you learned to regulate the amount of smoke you inhaled that you were able to tolerate smoking. As a chronic smoker, you probably smoke while you carry on other activities. In fact, every smoker we have worked with smoked in a variety of different situations, while taking part in a number of quite dissimilar activities. (Remember your smoking diary and your smoking pattern.) Smoking while you are engaged in other behaviors probably helps you distract yourself from the unpleasantness of your smoking habit.

Aversive smoking is designed specifically to (a) make you more aware of the natural unpleasantness of your smoking habit and (b) help reduce and perhaps eliminate the attraction of cigarettes. In addition, if it is used correctly, the aversive smoking procedure establishes vivid memories of smoke aversion that can be imagined when you are trying to avoid smoking later on.

The timing of the aversive smoking procedure—your schedule for using the procedure—has been carefully determined. It provides additional help, because it allows you to break the chains that bind smoking to situations.

Let us examine this issue of scheduling. You will reduce your smoking by half for three days. Then you will use the aversive smoking procedure on three consecutive days followed by a more gradual sequence thereafter. You should smoke only within these scheduled sessions; no other smoking should occur. In this way, you continue to smoke, still providing yourself with some nicotine, but only in one place and using a procedure that helps you make it highly unpleasant.

GRADUAL REDUCTION OR
COLD TURKEY?

In the preceding paragraph, we mentioned that there will be a set number of sessions for aversive smoking and that there should be no smoking at other times, especially in the usual circumstances. Many people try to compare aversive smoking to the more familiar concepts of gradual reduction or the cold-turkey approach.

Aversive smoking avoids the pitfalls of both of these procedures. First, the gradual-reduction method instructs you to slowly trim your smoking habit a cigarette at a time until you eventually have stopped all smoking. Schemes have been developed that usually begin with the easier smoking events and then work up to the more difficult or more highly valued. Unfortunately, all gradual-reduction methods share the common problem that they actually increase the value of each cigarette you smoke. By cutting back on the number of smokes per day, you make each remaining cigarette even more valuable: You actually increase your interest in and enjoyment of smoking. You have probably experienced this effect if you have ever tried to cut back on the number of cigarettes per day or per hour. You have probably found that each remaining cigarette becomes highly rewarding; you eagerly look forward to the next smoke. Obviously, because they make cigarettes more highly valued rather than devaluing the smoking habit, gradual-reduction methods are not likely to be effective, and research has proved this to be the case. Aversive smoking instructs you to stop all smoking outside of the aversive smoking session.

The second familiar method for quitting smoking is to stop all smoking abruptly—all at once. This method, the cold-turkey approach, tends to panic many individuals because they just cannot face going without ever smoking again. In addition, abrupt quitting probably increases the experience of withdrawal, because there is a drastic change in habitual behavior and a rapid halt to the body's absorption of nicotine. Aversive smoking gives you two to three weeks of continued smoking, but the setting and the manner of smoking are carefully controlled to make it easier to quit completely thereafter.

RAPID SMOKING OR
REGULAR-PACED AVERSIVE SMOKING?

There are two types of aversive smoking, and you will have to make a decision about which to use. Both procedures will cause you to experience considerable discomfort. In fact, they have to be unpleasant to work. One type, rapid smoking, calls for you to puff every six seconds until you cannot tolerate further smoking or until you have smoked three cigarettes. As you can probably imagine, puffing at that rapid six-second pace produces unpleasant reactions very quickly! Of course, that is the idea in smoke aversion—to make you more aware of the negative effects.

Rapid Smoking

The rapid smoking procedure has been extensively tested, perhaps more than any other available procedure for smoking control, and it has shown itself to be at least as effective as alternative procedures—and sometimes strikingly more effective! The best results from the reported research show 60 percent of volunteers in smoking clinics were not smoking six months after the end of the program.

Although it has recently been estimated that some 35,000 persons have used the rapid smoking procedure without any lasting ill effects, it is important to be conservative and careful in suggesting its use, especially in a self-help book like this. Rapid smoking presents some excessive risks for persons with a clear-cut history of cardiovascular or respiratory disease, because it stresses both of these important bodily systems. In addition, there are other reasons or precautions that should guide your decision about using rapid smoking, and we have included a medical self-screening questionnaire at the end of this chapter. As a final precaution, we suggest that you use the physican-approval form, also included at the end of this chapter, to check with your personal physician about your health history. Physicians often do not charge very much—if anything—for this assistance.

Regular-Paced Aversive Smoking

Instead of puffing so rapidly, you can choose to puff at a more normal rate of once every 25 to 30 seconds while you pay close attention to the unpleasant aspects of your smoking. The research evidence for the value of this regular-paced version of aversive smoking is not so clear as for rapid smoking but a number of reports have shown it to be a helpful tool for quitting. Of course, regular-paced aversive smoking must be done at a special time without distractions.

Audiocasette tapes that present the exact instructions and timing for both rapid smoking and regular-paced aversive smoking have been produced. These taped materials are one part of a *Comprehensive Smoking Cessation Program* which can be purchased through BioMonitoring Applications, Inc., 270 Madison Avenue, New York, N.Y. 10016.

SCHEDULING AVERSIVE SMOKING SESSIONS

You should pick days that allow you sufficient time to actually use the aversive smoking procedure faithfully. The entire session may take about 30 minutes, so make sure you pick times that are both practical and convenient. The

schedule should follow this pattern:
   one session daily for three consecutive days, then
   one session on each of three alternate days.
The following example should clarify this point about
scheduling.

Sample Schedule for Aversive Smoking

Session 1:   Session 4:
   Tuesday, March 7   Saturday, March 11
Session 2:   Session 5:
   Wednesday, March 8   Monday, March 13
Session 3:   Session 6:
   Thursday, March 9   Wednesday, March 15

What Do You Need for Aversive Smoking?

Fortunately, you do not need elaborate materials for
aversive smoking. Two packs of your preferred brand of
cigarettes, a slow-burning utility candle that allows you to
continue puffing without interruptions, matches, and an
ashtray. Many participants have found it helpful to have a
wastebasket with a plastic liner available for smoking sessions
just in case nausea and vomiting occur. It is NOT necessary
for vomiting to occur, however, for either form of aversive
smoking to be of benefit to you in your effort to stop smoking. Optional equipment includes a watch with a second
hand and a metronome to keep up the puffing tempo.

You will use what is called a negative sensation checklist
for every smoking session (see Figure 9). This form lists the
possible unpleasant experiences that can occur—and have
occurred—in aversive-smoking sessions. You should keep
this form in front of you throughout the smoking period to
help focus your thoughts on the experience of aversive smoking.

Figure 9

Negative Sensation Checklist for Aversive Smoking

SENSATIONS EXPERIENCED	SESSION 1		SESSION 2		SESSION 3		SESSION 4		SESSION 5		SESSION 6	
	Trial 1	Trial 2	Trial 1	Trial 2	Trial 1	Trial 2	Trial 1	Trial 2	Trial 1	Trial 2	Trial 1	Trial 2
dry mouth												
burning tongue												
dry throat												
burning lungs												
watering eyes												
sinking feeling in stomach												
feeling sick in stomach												
dizziness												
pounding of heart												
tingling at extremities												
face flushed												
headache												
feeling weak or faint												
nausea												
disorientation												
Rating of Unpleasantness (number from 1–7 from scale)												

First check off each of the sensations you experience. On the last line, rate the unpleasantness of the entire trial of smoking using the following rating scale:

1	2	3	4	5	6	7

Not at all   Moderately   Highly
unpleasant   unpleasant   unpleasant

Although you will not experience all of the sensations, you should pay close attention to the feelings produced in aversive smoking so that they can become vivid memories.

The Setting for Aversive Smoking

You should be alone, undisturbed, and facing a blank wall while you are following the aversive smoking procedure. Any distraction, such as television or radio can keep you from focusing all your attention on the unpleasantness of the immediate smoking experience. Select a room that is relatively small and that contains a blank wall, a chair, table, and a window that is not in your immediate view. The window allows you to remove the smoky air between smoking trials if this becomes necessary.

Some people select a bathroom, although this may present problems because of necessary interruptions. Other possible spots include a bedroom, garage, attic, den, and so on. Pick a room that best serves the purpose of allowing you privacy and no distractions.

Format of Typical Session

The following diagram (see Table 5) describes the format of a typical aversive smoking session. There are two trials, or episodes of smoking, that is, puffing according to the tempo described earlier, 6 seconds or 30 seconds. Between trials of smoking, there is a rest period which includes actual recuperation and reflection on the negative sensations experienced in the preceding smoking episode.

Rules for Aversive Smoking

Because it seems so simple, the aversive smoking procedure can be used incorrectly. Remember, the experience is designed to be very unpleasant for you. Many persons unwittingly change the procedure so that it is less unpleasant. That's understandable: After all, most of us work hard to avoid unpleasant things. But it is dangerous, because the whole procedure can be sabotaged, setting you up to remain a chronic smoker. To make sure that you are using the correct procedure, the following critical rules must be observed:

Rule 1. You must *avoid all smoking* except in the scheduled aversive smoking sessions. Keep a supply of cigarettes (two packs only) in the same place you have stored the other materials for your home treatment. All other cigarettes should be thrown out. Sign the personal contract (see Figure 10).

Figure 10

My Personal Contract for Nonsmoking
Between Aversive Smoking Sessions

I agree to avoid all smoking between my scheduled aversive smoking sessions. I realize it will be difficult and require my effort and careful attention. I understand that not smoking during these critical times will contribute to the overall chances for becoming a permanent ex-smoker.

_____   _____

(your name)   *(date)*

Table 5
General Procedure
For Aversive Smoking

Regular-paced aversive smoking		Rapid smoking (with physician approval)
	START OF SESSION	
Puff every 30 sec. (1 cigarette maximum to personal tolerance). Pay attention to unpleasantness. Recuperate from smoking period. Reflect on unpleasant experiences using negative sensation checklist.	Smoking Period #1 ↓ Rest period #1 5 min. ↓	Puff every 6 sec. (3 cigarette maximum to personal tolerance). Pay attention to unpleasantness. Recuperate from smoking period. Reflect on unpleasant experiences using negative sensation checklist.
Puff every 30 sec. (1-cigarette maximum to personal tolerance). Pay attention to unpleasantness. Recuperate from smoking period. Reflect on unpleasant experiences using negative sensation checklist.	Smoking period #2 ↓ Rest period #2 at least 5 min. ↓ *END OF SESSION* No more smoking until next scheduled session.	Puff every 6 sec. (3-cigarette maximum to personal tolerance). Pay attention to unpleasantness. Recuperate from smoking period. Reflect on unpleasant experiences using negative sensation checklist.

Figure 11
Physician Approval Form for Rapid Smoking

Dear Doctor:

I am trying to stop smoking and am following a program described in the book *Become an Ex-Smoker* by Brian G. Danaher, Ph.D., and Edward Lichtenstein, Ph.D. One part of the program that I can use, if you feel my physical condition allows, is an aversive smoking method that involves a small degree of risk. Of course, continuing to smoke involves considerable risk as well. I want to check with you in order to obtain your approval before I use the procedure.

One part of the program involves *rapid smoking,* and it has been designed to emphasize the negative effects of smoking. It calls for me to smoke rapidly (a puff every six seconds) and continuously until I cannot bear to take another puff or until I have smoked three cigarettes — whichever happens first. I may smoke up to three cigarettes in this fashion in the smoking episode. After a brief rest, I go through another trial of this sort. I self-administer as many as six sessions over the course of the program, although there is never more than one session on any one day. The rest of the program involves substitute behaviors and ways I can cope effectively with lingering smoking urges.

The rapid smoking approach has received perhaps the greatest research attention of any contemporary smoking treatment. Numerous controlled studies have found it to be at least as effective as alternative treatments — and sometimes markedly more effective. (See the review article by Brian G. Danaher, Ph.D., Research on rapid smoking: Interim summary and recommendations, *Addictive Behaviors* 1977, *2*). Its impact on participants' health has also been intensively examined. Researchers and practitioners have used rapid smoking on many thousands of persons without any lasting ill effects. The procedure does lead to considerable nicotine and carbon monoxide intake, which stresses the cardiovascular system. The risks are detailed in a recent review article by Edward Lichtenstein, Ph.D. and Russell Glasgow, Ph.D., Risks and safeguards in rapid smoking, *Journal of Consulting and Clinical Psychology,* 1977, *45*.

The program I am following prohibits the use of rapid smoking with individuals who have a history of heart or vascular disease, chronic obstructive pulmonary disease, or diabetes, or with women who are pregnant. In addition, it is recommended that no one over the age of 40 should use the procedure because cardiovascular risk increases with age.

You should know that rapid smoking is not the only procedure presented in the program that I can use. It does seem to be the most effective component, but I can turn to alternative, less stressful procedures if you think it best. I would like you to review my records, conduct any further examinations you may think necessary, and then indicate whether you think I have some condition that would preclude the use of the rapid smoking procedure.

_____

(participant's signature)

. . . .

To my knowledge, there are no medical contraindications to this patient's undergoing rapid smoking as described to me.

_____, M.D.   _____

(doctor's signature)   (date)

Rule 2. You should follow the aversive-smoking procedure until you reach your own personal limits or until you have smoked the maximum number of cigarettes, whichever comes first. Getting sick and vomiting will not improve the effectiveness of the treatment and should be avoided. Remember, this procedure is designed to supply you with a maximum experience of smoke aversion without your becoming sick.

Rule 3. Never undertake more than one aversive smoking session with two trials daily. (Follow your schedule.)

Rule 4. You must concentrate on the unpleasantness of the smoking experience if it is to help you stop smoking. It is natural and adaptive for us to tolerate unpleasantness by thinking distracting thoughts. But in aversive smoking, you will have to overcome this normal tendency and force yourself to concentrate only on the aversion you experience.

Rule 5. The last and the most important rule is that you must obtain permission from your personal physician prior to using the *rapid smoking* procedure. He or she should have the opportunity to read the technical summary and physician-approval form (Figure 11).

TECHNICAL SUMMARY ON RAPID SMOKING

This more technical section is designed to give you additional information on the effects of rapid smoking. The rapid smoking procedure, which calls for you to puff every six seconds, dramatically increases the level of nicotine and carbon monoxide in your system. Nicotine levels following rapid smoking are clearly higher than after normal-paced smoking, and they are related to an increase in heart rate. Increases in carbon monoxide reduce the oxygen-carrying ability of your blood. Both effects, then, place your cardiovascular system under some stress. Cardiovascular strain may be dangerous for individuals who have heart disease. For healthy individuals, however, this strain falls well within safe levels—perhaps comparable to the strain experienced in vigorous exercise. You should complete the self-screening medical questionnaire (see Table 6), which will help you make the decision about which treatment to choose.

But it is important to realize that risk is not a black-and-white issue. You or your physician may not be aware of the presence of some disorder that may be aggravated by the rapid smoking procedure. That is why you must consider the relative risks and benefits of rapid smoking. This treatment procedure appears to be the most powerful intervention to stop smoking, but other procedures in this book may be effective for you, too.

An even more technical review of the effects of rapid smoking is presented as a letter to your personal physician (see Figure 11). You should tear this section out of the book (or photocopy it if you prefer) and ask your physician to read it and approve your participation before you start. A review of the effectiveness of rapid smoking is contained in the appendix section at the end of this book.

Let us again emphasize that we are being very conservative in pointing out the possible risks of the procedure. You should know that it has been used with many thousands of smokers with few medical complications and no deaths. We believe that the risk is very small if you pass all the screening requirements. You may think that rapid smoking is pretty potent stuff. It can be, but remember that it is just intensifying the effects that every cigarette you smoke has on your body!

Table 6.
Self-Screening Medical Questionnaire

---

1. Have you *ever* had:
   (a) a heart attack? ——— yes ——— no
   (b) heart disease or heart trouble? ——— yes ——— no
   (c) frequent chest pains? ——— yes ——— no
   (d) diabetes or family history of diabetes? ——— yes ——— no
   (e) serious high blood pressure? ——— yes ——— no
   (f) emphysema? ——— yes ——— no
   (g) tuberculosis? ——— yes ——— no

2. Are you pregnant? ——— yes ——— no

3. Are you 40 years of age or older? ——— yes ——— no

If you answered yes to any of these, do *not* try rapid smoking.

4. Have you had or do you have:
   (a) shortness of breath when climbing stairs? ——— yes ——— no
   (b) decreased blood flow to your limbs? ——— yes ——— no
   (c) bronchitis? ——— yes ——— no
   (d) asthma? ——— yes ——— no

These are *possible* problems, depending on their frequency and intensity. You can go on to the next stage—seeking your doctor's approval—but you should discuss these symptoms with him or her.

SUMMARY

Two aversive smoking procedures that can help you stop smoking are described. One procedure called rapid smoking requires the smoker to puff once every six seconds until personal tolerance is reached or three cigarettes have been smoked. This rapid smoking procedure has shown considerable effectiveness, but it should not be used by everyone. (Suggested rules and limitations are outlined.) The second method called regular-paced aversive smoking calls for the smoker to puff every 30 seconds to tolerance or until one cigarette is smoked. Both aversive-smoking approaches prohibit all smoking outside of scheduled sessions. Rules, forms, and schedules for using aversive smoking are presented.

Checklist

———— Continue keeping track of smoking and urges in your smoking diary.

———— Continue practicing relaxation.

———— Read the technical summary on rapid smoking and complete the medical self-screening questionnaire.

———— Decide whether to use aversive smoking or methods described in Chapter 4 for quitting.

———— Consider obtaining your physician's approval for rapid smoking.

———— Follow the rules for the method you select.

section III

Remaining an Ex-Smoker (week 4 and beyond)

In the previous chapters you learned about the psychology of your personal smoking habits and some skills that helped you stop smoking—at least temporarily. Almost every smoker continues to experience smoking urges after stopping. In fact, many persons actually experience an *increase* in both the intensity and the number of smoking urges once they have stopped smoking. Unless you actively learn to cope with and attack these smoking urges, you will soon be drawn back into the smoking habit. It may be helpful to refer to your personal smoking graph for further details about what has happened to you since you stopped smoking (see Figure 5).

As you can see, when you were smoking, your urges were almost always followed by a cigarette (close to a 1:1 match). Once you succeed in cutting out all cigarettes, however, the urges usually continue—even increasing in daily intensity and frequency. While some persons seem able to gradually stop thinking about smoking altogether, most have to actively cope with these lingering smoke urges. Otherwise, it is back to satisfying these urges by smoking!

The ideal outcome to your effort to become an ex-smoker, of course, is the point at which both actual smoking *and* the smoking urges are reduced to zero. At this point, you will no longer be bothered by constant (pro or con) thoughts about smoking. You will be able to lead a normal life—but as an ex-smoker! (We know of some ex-smokers, however, who never entirely lose the urge, the occasional desire to have "just one." They must remain on the alert at all times, ready to cope with such an urge.)

This section on maintaining your nonsmoking habit describes, in specific detail, strategies you can use to help attack your lingering smoking urges. The strategies themselves will help you break up the long-standing links between your smoking habit and certain situations. Once these links are broken and new behaviors are developed to replace them, the intensity and, more importantly, the daily frequency of smoking urges will decrease.

Turning Point of Treatment!

The beginning of the section on maintenance presents a critical turning point in your self-treatment effort. You should continue reading the chapters in sequence if you have:

1. *stopped* smoking, or

2. *very substantially reduced* smoking.

The turning point becomes critically important if you have not been able to stop smoking as yet and are turning to this chapter for additional ideas on quitting. It is doubtful that the ideas presented in this chapter will help you. They are aimed much more at helping attack the smoking urges that remain, once actual smoking has at least temporarily stopped. As long as you continue to smoke, you will be strengthening the links—the associations—that this section attempts to weaken and break apart. Working both for and against smoking in this manner will only produce frustration and self-doubt.

We suggest the following two options if you are still smoking.

1. Return to the section on quitting and use some of the procedures described there. If necessary, use them again but in slightly different ways—specifically, restyle them to your advantage—based on what you have learned. If you have not already done so and have permission from your physician, switch to the more stressful aversive smoking procedure called rapid smoking. If these procedures still do not seem to help, then do this:

2. Turn to Chapter 11, "If You Can't Stop Smoking," for a discussion of options left open to you. As someone who is still smoking, you should not continue with the procedures discussed here because they are not designed for your needs; they are *maintenance* strategies for ex-smokers. What you need comes first: a scheme that will help you quit the habit. Then you will be ready to work on remaining a permanent ex-smoker.

chapter 6

Changing
the Smoking
Signals

Your smoking habit has been closely associated with numerous situations over the years. These close associations have produced links that almost compel you to think about smoking and create an urge to smoke during your usual activities and in routine places. Now that you are no longer smoking, these links begin to break up and new associations with *nonsmoking* activities grow. The problem for many people is that this process seems to take a very long time—so long, in fact, that many people are unable to continue their nonsmoking behavior.

But rather than passively sit back and hope for the best—that your smoking urges will dissipate on their own over time—you can *actively attack* these smoking urges. Then their intensity (attraction) and their frequency will be dramatically reduced. This chapter describes a set of helpful methods you can use to reduce the remaining smoking urges. Its purpose is to make changes in some of your daily routines that will maximize the chances of breaking the links between smoking and your activities.

YOUR PATTERN OF SMOKING URGES

Reviewing your smoking diary should reveal that some *new* patterns of smoking urges have developed since you stopped smoking. You should now see in your record unrewarded urges, that is, urges *not* followed by smoking. You may also see that your urges are more intense now (more of them in the 5 range). Your task is to begin to make sense out of your record of smoking urges. What patterns do you see? Do they cluster around mealtimes, or when you awake in the middle of the night or in the morning? Do they seem to be much stronger, even irresistible, once you have had a few drinks?

Consider the following example:

> MaryAnn, an assistant buyer at a department store, smoked about one pack of cigarettes each day. She was able to stop smoking completely when she used the rapid smoking procedure described earlier. Once she stopped, however, she noticed a marked increase in the number of smoking urges she experienced. In searching for a pattern to these urges by examining her smoking diary, MaryAnn learned that the strongest urges occurred when she awoke in the morning, when she had her coffee breaks at work, and when she arrived home and had a glass of wine before dinner. MaryAnn listed her major smoking signals as (1) "Getting up in the morning, in the bedroom;" (2) "Having coffee at 10:30 and 3:30 at work, usually with others around;" and (3) "Drinking wine at home after work at 6:00, usually with my husband."

See if you can identify your own pattern of smoking urges, and then list the urges in the spaces provided below, indicating times, places, and persons.

My Pattern of Smoking Urges

1. ————————————————————————

2. ————————————————————————

3. ————————————————————————

4. ————————————————————————

5. ————————————————————————

6. ————————————————————————

7. ————————————————————————

8. ————————————————————————

9. ————————————————————————

10. ————————————————————————

The times when you are most susceptible to intense smoking urges will be called smoking signals. Your personal signals may be activities, such as watching television, talking on the telephone, or eating out. Or you can think of them as places, such as your desk at work, your car, or your living room.

NONSMOKING SIGNALS

In addition to identifying your smoking signals, you should pay attention to those times and places that never prompt you to think about smoking. Some persons, for example, never consider smoking while in their boss's office at work, in a car, or in a bedroom. Others never or rarely smoke before noon. Whatever your reasons, you may have established certain times or places that have never been associated with smoking. Now that you have stopped smoking, you naturally find that you have no trouble at all at these times and in those places because the subject of smoking "doesn't even come into your head."

Returning to the example of MaryAnn, she found that she never smoked while in her car, when talking to particular nonsmoking friends, or while knitting. MaryAnn listed these three activities on her list of nonsmoking signals: (1) "Driving anytime, anyplace, alone or with others;" (2) "Talking to George T. or Linda G., anyplace; and (3) "Knitting anytime, only at home, when I'm alone." Once you have identified *your* list of nonsmoking signals, write them in the following spaces, again indicating times, places, and persons.

My Pattern of Nonsmoking Signals

1. ───────────────────────────────

2. ───────────────────────────────

3. ───────────────────────────────

4. ───────────────────────────────

5. ───────────────────────────────

6. ——————————————————————

7. ——————————————————————

8. ——————————————————————

9. ——————————————————————

10. ——————————————————————

SWITCHING SIGNALS ON YOUR URGES

Now that you have identified your personal smoking signals and your nonsmoking signals, your job is to actively start changing the smoking signals into nonsmoking signals. The method is to make changes in your routine so that you are using the nonsmoking signals to your advantage. Can you find a nonsmoking signal that you can use when you experience a smoking urge? If you can find a convenient signal, then you have a very effective tool in your effort to remain an ex-smoker. Consider the following example:

> Larry checked his smoking diary and found that walking and sitting in his car were nonsmoking signals, while lunchtime at work was a bothersome and attractive smoking signal. In an effort to change a smoking time into a nonsmoking time, Larry made the following plan: (1) He would drive his car to a park at lunchtime and eat in his car. (2) Once he had finished his lunch, he would take a walk around the park until he had to return to work. In this way, Larry was able to use patterns, which he had apparently established years earlier, to his best advantage now that he was trying to resist smoking urges.

Of course, it is not always possible to find nonsmoking signals to help replace your smoking signals as Larry did. When possible, of course, replacement is the best method. But at other times, adjustments in your usual activities can also help attack remaining urges.

ADJUSTMENTS IN SIGNALS

Any long-standing habit can be changed by making small adjustments in your routine. If you always read the newspaper when you get up in the morning—and if this is a strong smoking signal—then perhaps you should (a) sit in another chair to read the paper, (b) read the paper after breakfast rather than before, (c) take a shower in the morning rather than at night, and so on. The theme underlying these suggestions is that smoking signals can be undermined by small but important changes in your routine. Consider the following example:

> Louise had always smoked in bed just before she fell asleep at night and also every time she awoke in the middle of the night. This pattern had been long-standing and when she tried to stop smoking these sleep occasions emerged as powerful smoking signals. Louise changed her usual routine so that she allowed herself to lie in bed only when very sleepy— ready to immediately fall asleep. If she wanted to read, she would read in the living room on the sofa. The same personal rule was used when she woke up in the middle of the night: she would read in the living room until she was very sleepy. By making these changes, Louise was able to effectively shut off the smoking urges in her sleeping situation. At first, however, she had some difficulty trying to fall asleep without

thinking about cigarettes. But she began using her newly developed relaxation skills, and they distracted her from thinking about smoking and helped her fall asleep.

Notice that you are not asked to make *substantial* changes in your routine, because many people are simply unable or unwilling to alter their long-standing patterns of living. It is certainly not wise or helpful for you to stop doing many of the things you like to do: don't avoid parties or dinners in restaurants, even though they may act as smoking signals. You will have to cope with urges in those situations sometime, and you need to continue providing yourself some of the fun things in life as well.

Many ex-smokers may be able to weaken their smoking signals quite effectively with the two tools we have outlined thus far, that is, inserting nonsmoking signals and making slight adjustments. But there are also many persons who require more help with methods for situations that seemingly cannot be changed:

> Kathy was a traveling sales executive for a cosmetics firm. Her job required her to drive from site to site to complete sales promotions. For her, driving for what seemed to be endless miles on the road represented a strong smoking signal. Few adjustments could be made because driving was required in her job, and no nonsmoking signals seemed available.

When the situation cannot be easily changed, say, when the change disrupts one's routine or causes significant consequences, a possible solution is to identify and then employ *substitutes* for your smoking. Kathy, in the example, could take a bus instead of her car, but she might lose her job as a consequence. By doing something instead of thinking about smoking, you actually change the situation and thus begin to undermine the tie between smoking and the activity or situation.

Substitutes for Smoking

Previously we made the point that signals for smoking can be attacked by making use of your personal nonsmoking signals—in effect, *signal substitution*. Since this ideal method is not always practical, you need other strategies. Substitutes for smoking are nothing new. Almost every smoker has thought about and actually used a substitute for a smoking habit. In the present case, however, you are to identify your smoking signals and add some new activity that provides new circumstances. In this way the link between smoking and old circumstances can be effectively broken.

Adding activities is somewhat more difficult than it seems at first. Certainly you can add foods such as celery, carrots, and other raw vegetables. Perhaps sugar-free chewing gum might change the situation enough to undermine smoking signals. In the example, Kathy could eat celery sticks as she drives to her job. Of course, it is important to prepare food substitutes in advance because they must be available for rapid consumption.

However, food substitutes have at least two drawbacks. First, no matter how inventive you are, it can be repetitious to eat any significant amount of vegetables—and filling, too. Second, by increasing the amount of food you eat without any increase in physical activity, you run the risk of gaining weight—a common problem for persons who try to become ex-smokers. (A later chapter is devoted to the problems of weight control.)

There are many other substitute activities besides eating. For example, if you drive your car quite a bit and find it to be a smoking signal, you could sing along with the radio music or listen to new stations, or perform some minor but helpful isometric exercises at stop signs. Any modest changes in your routine will help, just as they helped this ex-smoker:

Gene found that every time he drove his car or sat in a business meeting he would experience a powerful urge to smoke. Instead of eating while driving, which was his first method for controlling urges, Gene began to listen to talk shows on the radio. And he found that this activity passed the time and seemed to help reduce his smoking urges. In addition, he began to do some tension-reducing relaxation exercises during his business meetings, especially in his legs and hands, and this new activity allowed him to continue to make sales without smoking.

In summary, good substitutes should be practical and not have negative side effects (like weight gain), they should satisfy the need apparently served by the cigarette (like stimulation or relaxation), and they should be incompatible with smoking. Realistically, you will not always be able to use an ideal substitute, but do your best to pick one. Think about possible substitute activities you could use and list them:

Possible Substitute Activities

1. _____

2. _____

3. _____

4. _____

5. _____

It is also quite possible to change what you are thinking about. The next chapter is devoted to a discussion of the critical skill of thought management.

Using Your Relaxation Skills

If you have practiced relaxing faithfully, you can relax your body and any set of muscles whenever you want. This is the time to use your relaxation skills to help you stay off cigarettes. There are several ways relaxation can help:

1. Relaxation can be used as a way to prevent the occurrence of smoking urges. By coping with stress before it builds into troublesome tension, you effectively prevent the rise of tension-related smoking urges.

2. Relaxation can also be used as a substitute response if you experience tension and a smoking urge. For example, let us say you are in a stressful job and experience an urge for a cigarette. Rather than smoke, you pause for a few moments, pinpoint the tense muscles, and relax your body. At the same time, you tell yourself that relaxation is a better way to cope with stress than smoking.

3. Withdrawal from smoking cigarettes often—but not always—leads to feelings of tension and irritability. So to cope with this possible reaction, you should schedule one or, preferably, two short relaxation sessions for yourself, to keep your withdrawal effects under good control. You can also think of these relaxation breaks as rewards for not smoking.

In the spaces provided, outline the strategies you will use in troublesome smoking signal situations. As you learn through experience which plans work, revise or update your list. Consider signal substitution, added activities, and relaxation—all the strategies discussed in this chapter.

Signal Situations   *My Personal Game Plan*

1. ——————————   ————————————

2. ——————————   ————————————

3. ——————————   ————————————

4. ————————————   ——————————————

5. ————————————   ——————————————

6. ————————————   ——————————————

7. ————————————   ——————————————

8. ————————————   ——————————————

9. ————————————   ——————————————

10. ————————————   ——————————————

SUMMARY

This chapter describes methods that should be used once you have stopped all or most of your smoking. The pattern of smoking urges, to be found in your smoking diary, provides the key for coping with lingering smoking urges. You are instructed to break up established patterns in your routine that involve smoking urges. Substitute activities and relaxation are suggested.

Checklist

———— Continue keeping track of smoking urges in your diary.

———— Use relaxation in the manner described.

———— Identify your personal pattern of smoking urges associated with times, places, and persons.

—— List your pattern of nonsmoking signals triggered by times, places, and persons.

—— List possible substitute activities.

—— Outline your personal game plan for resisting smoking urges.

chapter 7

Managing
Your Thoughts

Thinking comes so easily and spontaneously to most adults that it seems almost automatic, and therefore it may appear to be beyond our abilities to control. Yet brief reflection on your experiences in childhood both at home and in school produces a different story. Much of child training in social behaviors, or socialization, includes specific training in appropriate thinking. We are not merely referring to guidance on thinking "straight" or clean thoughts. Instead, we refer to instruction on how to anticipate consequences of your actions: "Look before you leap," or "If you do this, then that will happen," and the mental shortcuts used to add up numbers, remember lists of items, and recall information.

Much of what is considered mature has to do with people's skills in managing their thoughts and, hence, their actions in a variety of everyday situations. Because good thinking has so much to do with learning to manage your behaviors, it should come as no great surprise that becoming an ex-smoker requires specific instruction in more effective thinking.

This chapter outlines a number of cognitive, or thinking, strategies you should use to help resist lingering smoking urges and strengthen your resolve to remain an ex-smoker. In many ways, the notion of willpower has to do with having effective skills in managing one's thinking in problem situations. Because practicing new ways of thinking is something you can do on your own without anyone's knowledge—it's a very private event—you can get thorough practice in using these procedures to become a thinking ex-smoker! And, because thinking is done privately, it can be used in almost every situation in which you experience urges or temptations to smoke.

BEWARE: THOUGHTS CAN ENCOURAGE SMOKING

The most dangerous kind of thinking is that which directly undermines your goal to remain an ex-smoker. Such thoughts, or rationalizations to resume smoking, often develop without your really being aware of them. The first task of this chapter is to describe common rationalizations so you will be aware of them and can identify your own rationalizations for smoking. Once these are identified, the next step is to cope with them by means of effective strategies. Thus, the second part of this chapter outlines the specific strategies, with case examples, that will help you master your own thoughts.

Nostalgia

Some temporary ex-smokers begin to long for the times when they could smoke as if reminiscing about some long-lost friend. Nostalgic thoughts may go like this: "I remember when I could smoke while watching the football game in the cold" or "It sure was fun to light up a smoke while sitting around the campfire in late summer." The main feature of these mismanaged thoughts is that they imply that you have given up something important. If these thoughts lead to actually planning a return to the good old smoking ways, then they are important targets of better management early in your career as an ex-smoker.

Testing Yourself

A number of individuals become quite pleased with their success at stopping and act overconfident. Too often, though, this kind of thinking leads to self-statements, such as "I'll bet I could smoke just one and then put it down!" or "I'm stronger than most people, because I can pick up cigarettes and then lay them down without any problems." Curiosity also can be a problem: "I wonder what it would be like to smoke one cigarette." While it is certainly helpful to praise yourself for progress—we discuss self-praise later in this chapter—misguided confidence can produce a sense of daring yourself to test your limits. Unfortunately, these tests often confirm how tenuous the balance is in the early days and weeks of being a temporary ex-smoker. You are better off by admitting the challenge of remaining an ex-smoker and granting your adversary, the urge to smoke, a lot of power and influence.

Crisis

At times of crisis, many temporary ex-smokers say to themselves something like "I'll handle this mess better if I have a cigarette" or "I went through so much hell, I deserve a cigarette." Unfortunately, these hard times often seem to happen again and again, continuing to justify smoking. However, it is possible for these thoughts to be anticipated and counteracted. Times of crisis, though, present unique and dangerous points at which the ex-smoker often justifies a complete resumption of the smoking habit. The rationalization for starting to smoke in a crisis is the same used by the overweight person who justifies excessive eating by saying "It was a special occasion." Crises and special occasions have a way of becoming almost daily events.

Unwanted Changes

Many temporary ex-smokers worry that changes they feel may be associated with their nonsmoking. For example, many individuals, particularly women, are concerned that they are going to gain weight once they stop. Others are concerned that they are going to be irritable around friends, family members, or colleagues. Another common concern involves worrying over your ability to work effectively at home or at the office without cigarettes. All of these concerns can take the form of worrying along the following lines: "I think I'm beginning to gain lots of extra weight—maybe I'd rather look slim than be an ex-smoker," "I'm being very short and irritable around my family—maybe it's more important for me to be a good parent and spouse than it is for me to be an ex-smoker now," and finally, "I'm really not getting any work done these days since I've stopped smoking."

Some of the changes may occur, but we have included specific strategies that should enable you to cope with them and even prevent them from happening. By worrying about such things, however, you begin to persuade yourself that any negative change associated with stopping is caused by not smoking! Controlling these thoughts is critical and taking steps to manage your weight, relax around others, and continue working effectively at home or in the office can help lay these concerns to rest without worrying.

Self-doubts

This final type of self-statement that can undermine your efforts to remain an ex-smoker involves doubting your ability to succeed. The topic can be almost anything from nicotine addiction and lack of self-control to previous unsuccessful attempts to quit. The self-statements can take the following forms: "I'm really addicted to smoking; I can't control myself," "I'm one of those people who doesn't have any self-control," or "I tried to quit many times in the past, and none of these efforts really worked out; why should I expect this one to last!" Imagine how angry and righteous you might become if a neighbor said some of these doubting phrases to you in person! Yet you are saying these things to yourself and they can actually contribute to your return to smoking if not checked.

Now that we have described a number of resumption thoughts, it is time for you to examine your own thinking and identify your own resumption thoughts. In the section that follows, we outline a number of ways you can overcome this unproductive sort of thinking. For now, though, take some time to identify your rationalizations (nostalgia, testing, crisis, unwanted changes, self-doubts). Make a list of them in the spaces provided. List the most frequent or the strongest thoughts first. Use the extra space under each line to briefly describe each thought—especially its persuasiveness.

My Resumption Thoughts

1. Thought: —————————————————————

   Description: ————————————————————

   ————————————————————————————

2. Thought: ——————————————————————

     Description: ——————————————————————

——————————————————————————————

3. Thought: ——————————————————————

     Description: ——————————————————————

——————————————————————————————

4. Thought: ——————————————————————

     Description: ——————————————————————

——————————————————————————————

5. Thought: ——————————————————————

     Description: ——————————————————————

——————————————————————————————

6. Thought: ——————————————————————

     Description: ——————————————————————

——————————————————————————————

7. Thought: ——————————————————————

     Description: ——————————————————————

——————————————————————————————

8. Thought: —————————————————————

Description: —————————————————————

—————————————————————

It may help you to think about the kinds of mismanaged thinking we have outlined: nostalgia, testing, crisis, unwanted changes, and self-doubts. For most people it is not enough just to identify and describe each kind of mismanaged thought that can produce resumption. Actual step-by-step strategies, or game plans, need to be developed to overcome and eliminate these persuasive and powerful sources of trouble. The remainder of this chapter presents plans that have been used with success to overcome lingering mismanaged thoughts that all temporary ex-smokers experience.

PLANS TO ATTACK
MISMANAGED SMOKING THOUGHTS

There are various ways you can attack your negative thoughts about smoking. The following list of five methods provides convenient strategies for becoming an ex-smoker.

Challenging

The first suggestion we offer for overcoming mismanaged thinking involves a direct mental confrontation with the logic of your thoughts. In challenging your self-statements, consider the logic that is drawing you back to smoking. Here is a case in point:

George was well on his way to being a successful ex-smoker
when he began to think back on how enjoyable it had been to
smoke while relaxing after work. With this thought running
through his mind (nostalgia), he began to seriously consider
having just one cigarette a day to relax (testing and overcon-
fidence). He remembered the good times when he was a
smoker (nostalgia). Fortunately George recognized that this
pattern of thinking was directly undermining his motivation
to remain an ex-smoker. He wrote down a number of his
challenges on an index card and read them every time he
found himself thinking about resuming smoking. For example, he reminded himself that he could *not* have just one
cigarette without smoking more; he could use deep muscular
relaxation daily to unwind from work instead of smoking. He
reminded himself that he could still have good times without
smoking, because smoking had only been linked through
habit to having fun. Finally, George told himself that he
should not let thoughts like these continue to run through his
mind, because they were undermining his motivation.

This example shows how mismanaged thoughts can be identified, challenged, and effectively controlled. It also illus-
trates how resumption thoughts often occur in bunches
rather than alone.

Benefits of Nonsmoking

Some nonsmokers are not aware of the emerging positive changes associated with quitting. So it is useful at this
point to prompt you to think about personal benefits.
Thoughts about these benefits can be powerful ammunition
in your battle against rationalizations to resume smoking.
You can consider physical improvements (more stamina,
greater activities), economic benefits (more money available
for casual spending), and interpersonal improvements (increased attractiveness to others, congratulatory comments

from colleagues and friends), and so on.

To return to the example of George, he began to pay more attention to the fact that he felt more strength when playing tennis, that his girlfriend had remarked how proud she was of his progress, and that he no longer awoke coughing in the middle of the night. The emphasis on thinking about the emerging benefits helps you to see your hard work in a positive light. You must begin to pay attention to the positive features of nonsmoking instead of merely thinking about taking something away from your routine. More will be said about nonsmoking benefits in the next chapter.

Remembering Aversive Smoking

Another strategy that is ideally suited to the program presented in this book is specific recollection of smoking's unpleasant aspects. You may already have experienced some of the physiological effects of chronic smoking, as these often compel people to quit the habit in the first place (smokers' cough, upset stomach, headaches, shortness of breath, etc.). Think back to how you felt the morning after you smoked heavily: How did your throat feel and your mouth taste? Clear memories of these experiences can help you overcome some of the lingering smoking urges and combat the mismanaged thinking that pulls you toward resumption.

If you have tried aversive smoking, the experience itself should provide you with a wealth of vivid and highly unpleasant experiences associated with smoking. Remember these unpleasant experiences, using your imagination to actually "see" yourself feeling nauseous, for example. We suggest that you identify the powerful, unpleasant associations of smoking and list them in the spaces provided. It is helpful if you re-examine some of your negative sensation checklists from your aversive smoking sessions.

My Negative Smoking Thoughts

1. _____

2. _____

3. _____

4. _____

5. _____

6. _____

7. _____

8. _____

9. _____

10. _____

Distractions

Rather than confronting thoughts directly or thinking about either the benefits of nonsmoking or the unpleasant memories of smoking, you can simply divert your attention from any aspect of smoking. Putting smoking out of your head is, after all, the real goal of the treatment program. You may want to concentrate on pleasant, enjoyable subjects—vacation spot, relaxation, evening party date, etc.—that help you take your mind off smoking.

Barbara, for instance, loved to go to the mountains for her annual vacation. She was able to remember every turn in her favorite hiking trail. For distracting thoughts, Barbara recalled walking along that trail, seeing the special reminders of past good times. She was able to pick up anywhere she left off in conjuring up brief episodes of this distraction during the busy working day. Now make a short list of thoughts that you could use to help you avoid thinking about smoking.

Some Pleasant Thoughts to Use

1. _____

2. _____

3. _____

4. _____

5. _____

Self-rewarding Thoughts

The final strategy we recommend is reminding yourself of the successes and strengths you have already shown. There are a number of real accomplishments you have recorded in reaching this point in the treatment program. In our culture, however, statements about our accomplishments, if made out loud, are looked down on as being vain, egocentric, boastful, and conceited, But these positive self-statements can be made to yourself silently, and they can act as powerful incentives and guides to maintain your motivation. Consider the following example: Let us say you do not smoke in a situation where you formerly smoked, say, at a tavern or after a meal. You can think to yourself the following thoughts: "Good job! I don't have to smoke in that situation anymore because *I can manage my own behavior!*"

Everyone has personal phrases used to recognize a job well done. Too often, however, we are unaware of the exact nature of these private comments, and thus we cannot use them to help maintain nonsmoking and manage behavior. The first step for you is to identify your positive, self-rewarding thoughts so you can use them to help you continue being an ex-smoker.

My Self-rewarding (Congratulatory) Thoughts

1. _____

2. _____

3. _____

4. _____

5. _____

6. _____

7. _____

8. _____

9. _____

10. _____

HOW TO USE THESE STRATEGIES

You have learned which thoughts can contribute to a resumption of smoking and a number of strategies you can use
to cope with and eliminate mismanaged thoughts. Here are
some hints that will help you use the lists you have made in
this chapter:

1. *Post a chart of your most meaningful thoughts on attacking
   mismanaged thinking.* Pick a conspicuous place at home or
   in the office.

2. *Carry examples of these thoughts on index cards for easy reference.*

3. *Keep your list of helpful attacking thoughts as up to date as
   possible.*

At the same time, try to avoid launching into long
stretches of mental confrontation or reverie. The distraction
procedures should be quickly used, with the eventual goal of
eliminating thoughts about smoking or smoking urges. Of
course, these cognitive strategies should be used with the
procedures and strategies described in other chapters.

SUMMARY

Effective management of your thoughts is a key skill in becoming a permanent ex-smoker. Rationalizations encouraging resumption of smoking usually center on several topics,

including nostalgia, testing, crises, unwanted changes, and self-doubts. Several plans for directly attacking mismanaged thinking are described, including challenging, thinking about the benefits of nonsmoking, remembering unpleasant smoking experiences (especially if you used aversive smoking), distractions, and self-reward statements.

Checklist

—————— Continue to use your diary—but just for the few remaining urges.

—————— Use relaxation as necessary, along with other substitute activities.

—————— Fill in your list of resumption thoughts.

—————— Consider the emerging benefits of not smoking.

—————— List your negative smoking thoughts.

—————— List your self-reward thoughts.

—————— List some pleasant distracting thoughts.

—————— Use your plans for constructive thinking—perhaps with index cards or a chart on the wall at home or at work as reminders.

chapter 8

Benefits of Not Smoking

"Stop Smoking!"   "Kick the Habit!"   "Give up Cigarettes!"

Have you ever noticed that almost all the antismoking slogans and signs take a decidedly negative perspective? They tell you to do away with something you value and to change your habits by *subtracting* part of your usual routine. We believe that your success in becoming a permanent ex-smoker requires you to view your effort as both a negative and a positive one. Of course, you are trying to avoid smoking, and this means that you are trying to take away from your normal routine. The more positive slant to this activity is equally important, however. You are trying to become more health-conscious, more vigorous, and more sensitive to tastes and aromas. Moreover, you want to be a better model for your children and other members of your family. You are trying to develop new ways of behaving that are certainly more important to you than smoking cigarettes.

Maintaining a negative view of your efforts ("Stamp out the weed!") helps you only temporarily. To become a permanent ex-smoker you need to immediately begin paying attention to the benefits of your nonsmoking. This chapter is designed to help you learn more about the positive side of becoming and remaining an ex-smoker. It will also help you direct your activity so that you can see this perspective more clearly. In a way, we are encouraging you to think positively, but we realize that much more is needed. It is necessary to identify the actual benefits that you gain. Remember that we did the same thing in focusing on rationalizations about smoking again in the previous chapter. The key is to be *personal* and *specific*.

HEALTH BENEFITS

It should come as no surprise that your physical state improves as soon as you stop smoking. The effects of carbon monoxide and nicotine disappear from your system within hours after you have stopped smoking, and thus your body is able to handle increasing amounts of exercise without becoming fatigued. This is not to say, of course, that you will immediately be ready to run a four-minute mile or leap over tall buildings in a single bound! It would be miraculous indeed if fitness could be accomplished so easily. But you should be able to notice positive changes in your endurance once you have stopped smoking.

The effects will be more pronounced in those persons who exercise frequently. Increased exercise is actually a very satisfying and useful byproduct of becoming an ex-smoker. It is satisfying because you should be able to do more than before, and most people find this a beneficial, encouraging result. Increased activity provides you with a new interest that can focus your mind on new thoughts, new planning, and new interactions with people who share a concern about good health.

Before embarking on any strenuous exercise, you would be wise to discuss the matter with your personal physician or cardiologist, especially if you have a history of cardiovascular disease. Talking to your doctor also gives you the chance to describe your success at quitting smoking and maybe reap a little well-deserved praise! (Remember, however, that you cannot always count on others to be encouraging.)

Once you begin to notice specific improvements in your health as an ex-smoker, you should not let these pass quickly out of your mind. In fact, thinking about increased physical fitness can help you attack rationalizations about resuming smoking. (Remember the previous chapter!) To help you keep track of these important benefits, write down those features of your health˙and outlook that are linked to being an ex-smoker (using the positive benefits discussed in this chapter). Be as specific and personal as possible. Do not just write "Feel better." Instead, try to pinpoint the ways you feel better. For example, write "Don't cough in the morning anymore" or "Less winded after mowing the lawn on Saturdays." List these benefits below.

My Personal Benefits
from Being an Ex-Smoker

1. ————————————————————

2. ————————————————————

3.

4.

5.

6.

7.

8.

9.

10.

As you identify your personal benefits, you may want to spend some time consciously *thinking about them*. As we mentioned in the previous chapter, reflection on the emerging benefits can help you directly counteract the tempting rationalizations that draw you toward resuming smoking.

Of course, not everyone experiences immediate and obvious physical benefits from stopping smoking. For example, an avid tennis player who used to play three or four matches per week while smoking is not likely to notice an immediate change in his game. Likewise, someone who sits in business meetings all day and has led an equally inactive life at home scarcely notices any positive changes in fitness. At the extremes of fitness, then, obvious changes will be difficult to identify. The inactive individual may notice some increased stamina upon adding exercise activities to his or her normal routine. The message here is: Look for beneficial changes; but if you are not experiencing them, then you may need to increase your daily quota of activity. Do not worry and do not expect too much.

REGAINING YOUR SENSES

Many ex-smokers report that they experience an awakening of their senses of smell and taste. Some say they had forgotten that food tasted so good; others identify new aromas they had never smelled before. Some even become quite involved in preparing meals in new ways that improve taste and aroma. This kind of benefit, while certainly an improvement from most standpoints, can signal impending weight gain if some precautions are not taken quickly and effectively. Increased caloric consumption without any balancing increase in activity level to burn off those calories can cause weight gain.

Weight gain is often a problem for many ex-smokers, to the extent that some individuals actually resume smoking in the mistaken belief that smoking keeps them thin. Return of taste and smell sensitivity does not signal automatic weight gain, so you should be able to enjoy these changes while you continue to keep a balance of eating and physical activity. Consider whether you have experienced any awakenings in your taste or sense of smell since you stopped smoking. If you can identify personal and specific examples, then these should be written in on your benefits list.

PERSONAL CLEANLINESS

Now that you are an ex-smoker, try observing closely a few fairly heavy smokers. Do you notice an odor on their breath or clothes, especially wool clothing? You used to smell like that, too! We suggest you go to your closet and smell some of your old clothes. Then have them cleaned or washed, because you do not want to smell like stale smoke anymore. In the same way, you may want to inspect some of your furniture. Stuffed chairs and sofas pick up and retain cigarette odors; they can be aired or wiped with a disinfectant. Perform a similar inspection of your teeth and fingers. If your teeth have traces of nicotine stains, consider getting them cleaned. Improvements in your appearance and your house will further reward your efforts to remain an ex-smoker.

Try to phrase these benefits in personal and specific terms, and write them in on the benefits list. For example, you might write "My clothes no longer smell of horrible stale smoke" or "My teeth are as white as they have ever been now that I've stopped smoking." Remember to take a positive perspective as you develop these lists.

MONEY IN YOUR POCKET

One of the most immediate and impressive benefits of being an ex-smoker is found in the dollars that you save by no longer buying cigarettes and other smoking paraphernalia (lighters, ashtrays), and new clothes without holes burned in them. Because you have undoubtedly been a regular consumer of cigarettes prior to stopping, you are now—whether you know it or not—actively receiving a *salary* for being an ex-smoker! Unfortunately, not many people notice this fact because the money not spent on cigarettes goes into a common fund and becomes indistinguishable from other loose change. We argue strongly that you should make this salary or reward for being an ex-smoker more obvious through the following steps:

Step 1. You should immediately figure out the exact amount of money you used to spend on cigarettes by checking your pretreatment smoking diary. Once you determine the average number of cigarettes you used to smoke daily, you should calculate the amount of money this translated into each day and each week. Use the example below to help this calculation:

> Bob used to smoke two packs of cigarettes a day before he became an ex-smoker. He figured he was spending approximately $1.10 per day, or twice the cost of a pack, 55¢. He then figured he was spending $7.70 per week (daily total times 7), or about $33 per month on cigarettes. He put aside that money for two months and then bought a backpack and compass so he could enjoy hiking in the mountains.

Use the handy spaces in Table 7 to enter information on your own savings.

Table 7
Cost of Smoking to You

Packs smoked per day in the past
  × price per pack = $_____ .
                        (daily cost of smoking)

Daily cost × 7 days per week = $_____ .
                              (weekly cost of smoking)

Weekly cost × 4.3
  average weeks per month = $_____ .
                         (monthly cost of smoking)

Monthly cost × 12 months per year = $_____ .
                           (yearly cost of smoking)

You may be surprised to learn how much money this amounts to. By not smoking two packs per day you are actually earning a salary of approximately $400 per year!

Step 2. Now that you have figured out how much you used to spend on cigarettes each week, you can set this same weekly amount aside in a special spot (a corner of a drawer or a piggy bank, for example) where it can be safely stored. This is the method for paying yourself a salary for being an ex-smoker.

Step 3. Once you have begun to save your money in this way, it is time to think about how it can be spent. Simply having money around does not mean as much as spending it upon some valued activity. One ex-smoker paid for a family trip out of his savings. Another bought himself a tennis racket. Any valued activity will do as a reward for being an ex-smoker. Of course, putting the money toward a family outing spreads the wealth around, and this may be appropriate if you feel your family has contributed to your successful efforts. It is also particularly helpful to select some activity that involves exercise. Consider the earlier example of Bob.

For whatever reason, many ex-smokers are reluctant to spend the money on themselves, even if they have saved it as instructed in Step 2. It is important to go ahead and spend the money so you can actually feel rewarded for your work. So we provide a list in which you should write the activities or items that can be supported by your no-smoking salary.

Personal List of Ways to Spend No-Smoking Salary

1. _____

2. _____

3. ―――――――――――――――――――――――――――

4. ―――――――――――――――――――――――――――

5. ―――――――――――――――――――――――――――

6. ―――――――――――――――――――――――――――

7. ―――――――――――――――――――――――――――

8. ―――――――――――――――――――――――――――

Note: If you used a personal contract for quitting, you may want to put the deposit given back to you by the "banker" into your earnings from being an ex-smoker. In this way, you can quickly establish a sizable account for future self-rewards.

SUMMARY

Trying to become an ex-smoker can be viewed both negatively and positively. You are trying to cut out a part of your normal routine while you grow more health-conscious, more vigorous, and more sensitive to experiences of taste and smell, and become a better model for others as well. The positive side is too often overlooked. Composing a list of benefits helps you pay attention to the positive side of not smoking. In addition, the money saved should be used as your salary for not smoking.

Checklist

———— Keep diary if it is still useful.

———— Continue using substitute activities and thought-management procedures.

———— Complete the list of personal benefits of being an ex-smoker.

———— Figure out how much you save per month by not smoking and put that amount aside as your salary.

———— Complete the list of ways to spend that salary for not smoking.

chapter 9

Successful Weight Management

So many persons gain weight when they stop smoking that some believe it to be an unavoidable result. Weight gain is not a common problem in programs that provide specific counseling about careful weight management, however. And the available research evidence does *not* clearly indicate metabolic changes in people once they stop smoking. We are left to conclude that changes in eating behavior produce an increased caloric intake and result in weight gain. (See the Resource Appendix for a more detailed discussion of the metabolism versus eating behavior evidence.)

To maintain your weight when you stop smoking, you have to make sure that you do not compensate for not smoking by eating more food. The food you substitute for cigarettes must be carefully selected so that its calorie content is relatively low; a good example is raw vegetables. Of course, you should also avoid relying solely on food substitutes, because there are numerous other ways of coping with and eliminating smoking urges, as presented in the preceding sections of this book. Using food as a reward for not smoking is particularly dangerous, because it means that you are likely to gain weight and then feel even more deprived if you try to cut back on your eating.

FOOD QUALITY

Certain foods have more calories than others. You can calculate the calorie content of foods by reading package labels or a calorie booklet available at most supermarkets. As a rule, you should avoid eating foods that are high in calories, those containing excessive sugar, for example. By checking the ingredients on the label, you can tell if the food has a high proportion of sugar. The ingredients are usually listed in order of amount, with the largest amount first.

FOOD QUANTITY

Foods with only moderate calorie content cause weight gain if you consume too much. Episodes of "binge-eating" are the downfall of many persons. If you eat something every time you experience a smoking urge, you are particularly susceptible to erring in the quantity of food you consume. The key is not to rely on food as the only substitute, or even a primary substitute for smoking.

PHYSICAL ACTIVITY

Calories can be used up, or burned, through various kinds of physical activity. Of course, certain activities are very efficient users of energy, for example, jogging, rope-jumping, and bike-riding. Many other activities, usually not viewed as vigorous exercise, still consume energy and can assist you in your efforts to manage your weight. Examples are walking, gardening, climbing stairs, golfing, and housework. Finally, recreational activities like tennis or swimming burn up a moderate amount of calories and thus serve as ideal forms of weight-control measures. Be sure that you consult your personal physician before you try to engage in any very strenuous activity. As a general rule, it is best to start slowly and then gradually find a level of activity that fits your stamina and routine.

SPECIAL PROBLEMS
OF EX-SMOKERS

As has been mentioned in this chapter, ex-smokers have special challenges when it comes to managing eating and weight. Many ex-smokers report that their increased sense of taste and smell makes food deliciously tempting. Using food substitutes for cigarettes can present serious problems. On the other hand, ex-smokers also report an increased interest in healthful activities that use up calories, too. Consider this example:

> Susan had resisted all smoking urges for almost two weeks when she first noticed she had gained almost five pounds. She

quickly reviewed her eating habits and found that she had been avoiding urges by not eating her usual low-calorie lunch but instead had been eating fruits and a little candy in midafternoon. In checking her recent activity level, she did not find any increases that would burn up these added calories. After two to three weeks of replacing high-calorie foods with raw vegetables in the afternoon and walking an extra 15 to 20 minutes per day, Susan was able to bring her weight back down to its usual level while remaining an ex-smoker.

It may be important for you to keep track of your weight as you make the effort to become an ex-smoker. You may also want to keep some notes on the quantity and quality of your eating and on your physical activity. If you experience some weight gain, make some adjustments in the balance of the calories you take in and the calories you burn up.

YOUR VIEW OF WEIGHT GAIN

If you do gain some weight, examine what this means to you. Be sure that your concerns about weight are not rationalizations for resuming the smoking habit you just worked hard to quit. Remember, many successful ex-smokers gained some weight at first but then lost it again without picking up cigarettes. It is easier to lose extra pounds than to stop smoking again!

Let us consider what you should do if the measures we have suggested do not help you lose weight. At that point you have to evaluate the relative cost of a few extra pounds versus resumption of the smoking habit. You may be concerned about your appearance but it is important to remember that smoking affects how you look, too. Scientific evidence shows that smoking is clearly more dangerous than a few extra pounds. In terms of cost, smoking is by all measures the behavior to avoid.

The points raised in the previous paragraph may put your decisions in some perspective and give you the added patience needed to avoid smoking while you employ other resources for weight management. To help you find reading material, we have included a list of weight-management references under "Smoking and Weight Gain" in Part A of the Resource Appendix, "Common Questions about Smoking."

SUMMARY

Problems with using food as a substitute for tobacco are highlighted. Calorie content (food quality) as well as extent of eating (food quantity) are discussed in terms of how you can manage your weight. The importance of physical activity is stressed. These special problems and your view of them are critical to maintaining nonsmoking over time.

Checklist

————— Evaluate the present quality of food in your diet.

————— Evaluate the present quantity of food you eat.

————— Evaluate your daily amount of physical activity.

————— Consider your thoughts about weight gain.

————— Make adjustments in quality, quantity, exercise, and thinking in order to avoid weight gain.

chapter 10

Planning Ahead

Many ex-smokers find that their smoking urges have almost completely disappeared 3 to 5 weeks after they quit the habit. Some persons report that they occasionally think about smoking (the subject), but they do not actually think about wanting to smoke (the activity). But people's experiences vary considerably in this matter of lingering smoking urges; you may find that not all your urges have disappeared by the fifth week or that new smoking urges have appeared in certain situations.

Smoking urges will linger or reappear in those situations that have been strongly associated with smoking in the past. Some of the adjustments you have made in your usual routine may not have been sufficient, or you may need to work further at managing your thoughts. Smoking urges can reappear in those situations that you have not encountered recently. If you suddenly find yourself in a situation in which you have not practiced nonsmoking, you may very well experience an urge to smoke. There may also be temptation situations that do not arouse a smoking urge but that can still be troublesome; these usually involve drinking alcoholic beverages.

There are two basic strategies to keep in mind for these infrequent and somewhat unexpected times when avoiding a cigarette may be a problem. First, you should try to anticipate the problem times, plan ahead, and prepare for them. Second, you need to know what you will do if you do have just one smoke.

ANTICIPATING THE UNEXPECTED

Even though people's experiences are often quite different, our clients have shown us some general patterns of particularly troublesome times that you need to think about and prepare for. After we outline our list, we give you some space to make a list of what you predict will be your personal problem times. Then you will have to design your personal coping program. Think about your plans. Will they be practical? Review your plans occasionally so that they will be ready to use when needed.

The Crisis

An unexpected and upsetting event, such as a car accident, divorce, financial failure, etc., occurs. You may experience an intense need to smoke. You may even tell yourself that because of the misfortune that has befallen you, you *deserve* the comfort of a cigarette—that you should not be expected to deal with the crisis while you have to fight your craving for cigarettes. Mismanaged thinking of this type rather quickly encourages you to resume smoking. Instead, you should use relaxation skills and distractions to effectively cope with the crisis without smoking. Fortunately, crises usually do not happen frequently, but this also means that you have relatively few chances to learn how to cope with the stresses without smoking.

The Reunion

Getting together with smoking friends, family members, and colleagues at work may present some very real temptations to resume smoking. This is particularly true if you have not seen these people since you stopped smoking. You may have to consider how you will announce that you have stopped smoking or how you can politely turn down an offer for a cigarette. Even without these verbal messages, you may feel a very strong sense that something is missing when you have a reunion, reflecting the fact that smoking was associated with many aspects of your social behavior. As before, you will have to prepare for these troublesome times by having substitutes available, managing your thoughts, and practicing your statements in advance.

The Tavern

Another troublesome time can occur when you are in a tavern or bar or perhaps at a party in someone's home where you are drinking alcoholic beverages and a lot of people are smoking. Not only is this situation strongly conducive to smoking, but the alcohol reduces your ability to resist by making it easier to rationalize that it is all right to have just one cigarette.

Since this situation often presents problems, plan ahead and develop some coping strategies that will help you through them. One helpful strategy is to avoid drinking very much for the first few social occasions so you can gradually adjust to drinking and partying without smoking. Some persons carry around a small card that helps to remind them of the negative experiences of aversive smoking, the emerging benefits of not smoking, and so on.

Your List of Troublesome Times

We have listed a few of the more common situations that can cause trouble for persons who have avoided smoking for some time. Some of our examples may suggest situations that you will have to watch out for as well. Write down some of your ideas in the spaces listed below. Be as specific as you can: Indicate the likely time, person, and place as well as the coping strategy.

1. ————————————————————————————

    Coping strategy: ————————————————————

2. ————————————————————————————

    Coping strategy: ————————————————————

3. ————————————————————————————

    Coping strategy: ————————————————————

4. ————————————————————————————

   Coping strategy: ——————————————————

5. ————————————————————————————

   Coping strategy: ——————————————————

SUPPOSE YOU DO SMOKE

If you give in during one of the situations just described, the cigarette may not taste very good and you may feel guilty about having smoked. But this is a critical turning point. There is no reason that one cigarette or even one puff on a cigarette should make you a habitual smoker again. The nicotine you absorb from that brief experience is not enough to chemically draw you back into smoking. The way you think about having slipped will largely determine whether you (a) use the event as a learning experience demonstrating that you will have to take more care in coping with smoking urges and preparing for unexpected events, or (b) rationalize to yourself that one cigarette means that you have fallen off the wagon and will resume your smoking habit. Pay attention to your thinking at this critical time; it may be worthwhile for you to think about how you would react *in advance*. We are not giving you permission to have that one cigarette or one puff just to test yourself, however. But remember, one smoke does not make you a smoker again. Also remember that you should try very hard to avoid smoking.

SUMMARY

Many smokers may be troubled by lingering smoking urges or urges that reappear long after they have stopped smoking. The association between smoking and these troublesome times is stressed as is the theme for preparing for possible events that might encourage you to resume smoking. Thinking about what a smoke would mean to your effort to become an ex-smoker is suggested.

Checklist

——— Complete the list of troublesome times.

——— Consider how you would handle smoking one cigarette.

section IV

Decisions and Information

Throughout this book you have learned new methods for solving the problems associated with becoming an ex-smoker. You have learned how to identify important patterns in your smoking habit. You have also learned ways to help you quit smoking and overcome lingering smoking urges.

This section of the book discusses some important decisions you may have to make if you have not stopped smoking, and it asks you to report on your personal experience in using the program.

If you have not completely quit smoking by this point in the program, you will have to decide whether to remain a controlled smoker or wait to use the program again at some later time. Of course, you also have the option of enrolling in another smoking cessation program, and alternative programs are briefly suggested.

If you have successfully stopped smoking, you should avoid stopping all of your work abruptly just because you have reached this section in the book. As mentioned in Chapter 10, you should plan ahead for possible problems and have effective plans ready for instant use. You may also have to continue using strategies to cope with any remaining smoking urges. Solving present and future problems will continue, then, no matter how successful you have been up to this point in the program.

Everyone who uses this book has important personal experiences and reactions. A feedback information form has been included at the end of this section to give you the chance to report on your experiences and to make suggestions for improvement.

chapter 11

If You Can't Stop Smoking

No smoking cessation program can guarantee 100 percent effectiveness. Despite hard work and careful attention to details, you may still find yourself smoking. If you reach the point where you feel the need to stop trying for a while in order to reevaluate your current status as smoker or ex-smoker, then we suggest you consider several major issues.

REMAINING A CONTROLLED SMOKER

Even if you have not stopped smoking completely, you have probably significantly reduced your daily consumption of cigarettes by the time you have reached the end of this treatment program. It is certainly true that the risks of smoking are related directly to how many cigarettes you smoke per day. Unfortunately, smokers who cut down actually compensate for the loss of nicotine by inhaling more deeply than before.

Remaining a controlled smoker means that you will probably have to continue working with many of the strategies described in this book. One thing is clear: Without working at it very hard and very consistently you are likely to resume smoking again at your original level. In fact, the great majority of smokers who cut back dramatically and try to remain at the reduced level end up smoking at their former level. To avoid this possibility, we strongly urge you to continue keeping track of your smoking behavior—both urges and actual smoking—while you use some of the urge-coping strategies outlined in Section III.

RECYCLING THE PROGRAM

After a period of time, you should make another assault on your smoking habit. Begin again with the first section of the book, and use what you learned in your first attempt as ammunition for your second attack. You will have to make records again, because subtle changes may have emerged in your smoking patterns.

The timing of your next attempt to become an ex-smoker should be carefully planned. If you found that specific time-consuming pressures prevented you from really applying all your efforts and attention to the first assault on the smoking habit, then pick a time when your life is a bit more calm and the setting is more conducive to the necessary hard work. For example, some smokers have been unable to stop smoking at the time of divorce proceedings, death of a family member, major change in jobs, relocating in a new community, or pending retirement. Once the emotional trauma of personal crises has passed, it may be more appropriate for you to begin working on your smoking program again.

Your commitment to quit should be clearly examined before your next attempt to stop smoking. Carefully review your reasons for and against becoming an ex-smoker. You may need more personal and persuasive reasons for quitting before you try again.

Support for your program may also have been inadequate in your first attempt to become an ex-smoker. Many smokers find that group programs provide both the needed structure and the social support that help motivate them and hence increase their chances for long-lasting success. As was mentioned in the preface, this book can be used in the context of a group program, and this may provide another option for you. If you cannot find a group smoking cessation program, then you might want to organize one at work or in your community. Self-help groups can perform a valuable service in this regard. Too often we underestimate the power of a well-organized effort of persons to help themselves and others.

You may also want to try another approach. It is certainly possible that you will find a better or more effective match with an alternative smoking program. Table 8 presents a list of alternative treatment resources that you can look into. Many of these alternative programs actually employ the ideas and strategies that are outlined in this book. For that reason, this book should be a helpful guide and a complementary resource.

Table 8
Alternative Treatment Resources
For Controlling Your Smoking

Societies and Associations (local and state offices listed in phone book)
American Cancer Society
American Heart Association
American Lung Association
YMCA

Inexpensive Smoking-control Programs
Five-day programs sponsored by Seventh Day Adventist Church
Cancer society quit clinics
University research clinics

Private, Profit-making Programs
Schick Centers for Control of Smoking/Weight
SmokEnders
Smoke Watchers

Professionals
Physicians (private and as part of hospital programs)
Psychologists
Public-health workers
Nurses

HOPELESS, CHRONIC SMOKER?

Whatever you do, if you reach the point of not being able to stop smoking, you should *not* fall into the trap of labeling yourself a hopeless smoker. Labels like this really are best viewed as examples of unproductive self-statements or thinking. They are dead ends that do not help you direct your

Figure 12
Feedback Questionnaire

General Instructions: This questionnaire is designed to assess your experience with this book on smoking control. It asks you to give some descriptive information and then some details about your success or failure in becoming an ex-smoker. You do *not* have to put your name on the questionnaire.

1. Male or female _____
2. Age _____
3. Reason for buying book: ☐ to stop smoking
                                ☐ for academic study
                                ☐ to use with others
                                ☐ other: _____
4. How many cigarettes did you smoke each day before treatment? _____
5. What is the longest time you have gone without cigarettes *before* using this book? _____
6. How many cigarettes are you smoking now each day? _____
7. If you are not smoking now, how long has it been since you
     used the book: _____ years _____ months _____ days
     stopped smoking: _____ years _____ months _____ days
8. For each of the following topics, please indicate the portions of the program you completed and how helpful they were to your efforts to become an ex-smoker. (Use the scale from 1 to 7; 1 = not at all helpful and 7 = extremely helpful.)

	Read Completely	Used the Strategies	Helpfulness Rating
relaxation (Chapter 3)			
nonaversive methods (Chapter 4)			
aversive smoking methods (Chapter 5)			
changing signals (Chapter 6)			
thought management (Chapter 7)			
benefits from not smoking (Chapter 8)			
weight management (Chapter 9)			

9. What reactions did you have to the Resource Appendix section? _____

_____

_____

10. Any other comments? ————————————————————————— ——

——

11. How would you improve the treatment program? (This sections is for your
general comments) ——————————————————————————

——

CUT QUESTIONNAIRE OUT OF BOOK ALONG THIS LINE

——

FOLD

FOLD
——

place
first–class
stamp
here

Brian G. Danaher, Ph.D.
Stanford Heart Disease Prevention Program
Stanford University Medical Center
Stanford, California 94305

Staple or tape here, and drop questionnaire in mailbox.

energies elsewhere. Be careful to avoid such thoughts. Instead, continue your efforts to become an ex-smoker. Many smokers reach their goal of total abstinence on the third, fourth, or later attempt!

FEEDBACK TO US

We would like to hear about your experiences so we can improve later editions of this book. You can help by taking the time to fill out the feedback questionnaire (Figure 12) at the end of this chapter and sending it to the address indicated. This will enable us to make improvements based on your experiences with the program. As new findings emerge from research and as we gain even greater experience with the self-help version of the program, we can provide more effective and enduring treatment instructions.

section V
Resource Appendix

The final major section of this book presents a detailed discussion of selected important issues in smoking cessation. We hope to stimulate an understanding of some of the complexities in each of the topics covered. The level of this discussion is distinctly more technical than that found in the preceding self-help section. Technical references from the clinical literature have been included in order to facilitate continued investigation by interested readers.

The first part of this appendix can be described as a discussion of "everything you've always wanted to know about smoking but didn't know who to ask." While the word "everything" is presumptuous, we have selected key questions that have been frequently asked by clients in our smoking-cessation programs. Specific information—summaries of the

major studies in the literature—as well as some of the con-
troversies are included. The topics are less harmful methods
of smoking (alternatives to complete abstinence?), pharmacological (drug) interventions for smoking control, hypnosis as smoking treatment, additional risks of smoking during pregnancy, and the link between smoking cessation and
weight gain.

The second appendix section provides the big picture of
the growing support for smoking-control action. Broadening
concern is highlighted by discussion of the emerging role of
health professionals, the primary prevention of smoking
among young people through school health programs, smoking control efforts found in occupational or work settings,
and legislative restrictions on smoking behavior.

The final part of this resource appendix describes the
empirical research evidence for the various behavioral
strategies suggested in this book. A number of intriguing
behavioral approaches to the modification of smoking behavior are outlined, and the most recent research findings
are presented. Past, present, and future trends are also described.

appendix A

Common Questions about Smoking

HYPNOSIS AS AN AID TO STOPPING

Q: Can hypnosis cure my smoking without all this effort and strain?

A: The evidence suggests that hypnosis does not eliminate the need for effort and by itself may not be helpful to most people.

The smoking-control literature contains a large number of case reports but disappointingly few controlled trials of hypnosis. The plentiful reports frequently herald very effective results, indeed, some of the most effective in the literature (for example, Nuland & Field, 1970, and Spiegel, 1970).

Unfortunately, most hypnotic programs have used complex and poorly described procedures. The rudiments of controlled research methodology have been lacking. There are no controlled studies that compare hypnosis and alternative interventions (Orne, 1977). Moreover, the literature of hypnosis has not presented any comprehensive theoretical orientation. All of these inadequacies have produced "a rather chaotic approach to smoking" (Johnston & Donoghue, 1971). It is easy to agree with Johnston and Donoghue's 1971 summary conclusion that "alone or in combination with other approaches, hypnosis has not been demonstrated to be effective."

The actual procedures included in hypnosis interventions for smoking have frequently involved directed imagery, which attempts to link the smoking habit with images of highly unpleasant, aversive experiences. Deep muscular relaxation also seems to have been a part of the method for inducing the hypnotic state. Hypnotic suggestions of reduction or abstinence have been rather common. Many of the reports in the literature have described office-based programs, although self-directed applications of hypnosis have appeared (LeCron, 1964). In self-hypnosis, there has been an emphasis on the influential role of new, usually positive ways of thinking.

Hypnosis can be viewed in terms of the operations that it involves (Barber, 1969). It can be instructive, therefore, to examine the actual procedures included in hypnotic interventions for smoking. For example, directed imagery procedures linking smoking to unpleasant experiences and thoughts have been used in extant forms of aversion therapy (Lichtenstein & Danaher, 1976) and are the characteristic interventions found in covert sensitization (Cautela, 1971, 1975). Both relaxation training and self-instruction have been reported in behavioral cessation programs (Bernstein & McAlister, 1976, and Cautela, 1975). Posthypnotic suggestions can be viewed as examples of contractual management (Hodge, 1976) similar to those described in behavioral research. Until some hitherto unidentified unique component of hypnosis is found to be critical to producing cessation, the procedures listed above can be more productively considered as examples of various behavioral intervention strategies suffering from markedly inadequate design methodology.

References

BARBER, T. X. *Hypnosis: A scientific approach*. New York: Van Nostrand Reinhold, 1969.

BERNSTEIN, D. A., & MCALISTER, A. L. The modification of smoking behavior: Progress and problems. *Addictive Behaviors*, 1976, *1*, 89–102.

CAUTELA, J. R. Covert conditioning. In Jacobs, A., & Sachs, L. B. (eds.), *The psychology of private events*. New York: Academic Press, 1971, pp. 109–130.

CAUTELA, J. R. The use of covert conditioning in hypnotherapy. *International Journal of Clinical and Experimental Hypnosis*, 1975, *23*, 15–27.

HODGE, J. R. Contractual aspects of hypnosis. *International Journal of Clinical and Experimental Hypnosis*, 1976, *24*, 391–399.

JOHNSTON, E., & DONOGHUE, J. R. Hypnosis and smoking: A review of the literature. *American Journal of Clinical Hypnosis*, 1971, *13*, 265–272.

LECRON, L. M. *How to stop smoking through self-hypnosis*. N. Hollywood, Calif.: Wilshire Press, 1964.

LICHTENSTEIN, E., & DANAHER, B. G. Modification of smoking behavior: A critical analysis of theory, research, and practice. In Hersen, M., Eisler, R. M., & Miller, P. M. (eds.), *Progress in behavior modification* (vol. 3). New York: Academic Press, 1976, pp. 70–132.

NULAND, W., & FIELD, P. B. Smoking and hypnosis: A systematic clinical approach. *International Journal of Clinical and Experimental Hypnosis*, 1970, *18*, 290–305.

ORNE, M.T. Hypnosis in the treatment of smoking. In J. Steinfeld, W. Griffiths, K. P. Ball & R. M. Taylor (eds.), *Proceedings of the 3rd world conference on smoking and health*. Washington, D. C.: U.S. Government Printing Office, 1977. Pp. 489–507. (DHEW Publication No. NIH 77–1413)

SPIEGEL, H. A single-treatment method to stop smoking using ancillary self-hypnosis. *International Journal of Clinical and Experimental Hypnosis*, 1970, *18*, 235–250.

LESS HARMFUL WAYS OF SMOKING

Q: Are there other ways I could continue to smoke and still reduce the danger?

A: This is a controversial question, but no safe and practical methods of smoking have been found as yet.

A growing number of researchers and organizations in smoking and health have focused their interest on the development of less hazardous methods of smoking. The belief that risks associated with cigarette smoking can be reduced without complete abstinence is based largely on epidemiological evidence that closely relates harmful components of the smoking habit with eventual disease and disability. Enthusiasm for this line of inquiry has been stimulated further by the admittedly disappointing results obtained in structured treatment programs and in public health campaigns. Moreover, the search for less harmful ways of smoking has been pragmatic in spirit: "In science, as in so many areas of life, while striving for the ideal, one must usually settle for that which is realistic" (Wynder, Mushinski, & Stellman, 1976, p. 11). The tobacco industry has financed substantial research and development in this area—not surprising, because it has a vested interest in the evolution of more acceptable and less hazardous smoking products.

The search for less harmful smoking has taken several distinct directions, from the changes that can be made in tobacco products to recommended changes in smoking habits to reduce risk. These important topics will be described in detail. While changes can be made independently of each other, targets for reducing the risks from smoking do have a pattern of influence, so changes in one factor may interact with the effects of other factors. This point is made in Figure 13; factors described in the outer ring can override those factors described by the inner rings.

Figure 13
Targets for Safer Smoking

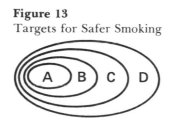

The factors include (A) agricultural methods, (B) tobacco composition, (C) cigarette design, and (D) smoking habits.

Changing the Tobacco Product

Epidemiological research has identified at least three critical ingredients in tobacco smoke that are associated with eventual disease and disability. The constituents and associated diseases are as follows: (1) tars—lung cancer; (2) carbon monoxide and nicotine—cardiovascular disease; and (3) hydrogen cyanide (HCN)—chronic obstructive lung disease, including emphysema. Hydrogen cyanide retards the cleansing function of the cilia in the lungs, which therefore reduces effective respiratory function (Ross, 1976). Highly sophisticated techniques have been developed to change the tobacco used in cigarettes so that the hazardous ingredients are substantially reduced.

The kind of tobacco used in the manufacture of cigarettes can be carefully selected through *agricultural methods*. Controlled breeding and hybridization can yield strains of tobacco that are exceptionally low in some of the harmful ingredients or those substances that later decompose into dangerous ingredients when burned. The use of certain pesticides and fertilizers during the tobacco growth period can also be carefully selected and applied in order to minimize the absorption of harmful compounds.

Once the tobacco is harvested, its *composition* can be radically changed to further reduce the potential hazard. Special processes such as freeze-drying have been used for this purpose. For example, tobacco can be broken down mechanically until it resembles a paper product; then chemicals are added or removed prior to returning the tobacco-like product to a more palatable form. These changes in tobacco's physical structure through reconstitution permit increased control over the rate of combustion, which, in turn, provide final control over production of particles and condensing gases.

So-called flavor enhancers can be added to increase the attractiveness of the processed tobacco product. An extensive research and development project is currently under way at the National Cancer Institute to pinpoint attractive flavors that can be added to the transformed cigarette products (National Cancer Institute, 1976a, b). It is important to note that the flavors being tested do not necessarily attempt to recapture the original taste of the tobacco unreconstituted; instead, the enhancers may be any attractive flavors.

When the reconstituted tobacco is ready for processing

and final packaging, the *design* of the cigarette envelope itself can facilitate the reduction of risk. The filter tip is the most common example of design change. Filtration mechanically lowers the usual levels of tars and nicotine that are absorbed into the body. The more complete the mechanical filtration, however, the more effort the smoker must exert to inhale the smoke. Vented filters that allow the entry of outside air have been developed as one possible solution; they also allow some carbon monoxide to escape and reduce the overall concentration of smoke. Chemical additives in the filter can neutralize some of the harmful ingredients and can aid in filtration without increasing the mechanical resistance.

Behavioral Aspects

Risk can be reduced by altering the normal method of smoking. A number of specific types of behavioral changes have been recommended: noninhalation, taking fewer puffs and leaving longer butts, changing to low tar-low nicotine brands, removing the cigarette from the mouth between puffs, reducing consumption (fewer cigarettes smoked per day), and changing to cigars or pipes (World Health Organization, 1975, and Wynder & Hoffmann, 1972). The guiding principle behind these behavioral recommendations is *to inhale as little as possible and to make what is inhaled as harmless as possible*. Early efforts to teach smokers controlled smoking are now being explored systematically (Frederiksen & Peterson, 1976).

Not all of these recommended changes in smoking behavior have met with support in the research community. In fact, much controversy surrounds some issues. Consider the recommendation to switch from cigarettes to pipes or cigars. Early reports cited epidemiological evidence showing lower morbidity and mortality statistics for pipe and cigar smokers.

One self-help book (Chesser, 1963) provided a practical step-by-step guide to adopting pipes or cigars as safer alternatives to smoking cigarettes. However, the most recent research has revealed that smokers who switch tend to continue inhaling the smoke and actually expose themselves to higher concentrations of identified harmful ingredients in smoke! Russell (1974) has made the distinction between primary and secondary pipe and cigar smokers to describe those individuals who have smoked only pipes or cigars as opposed to those smokers who have made the switch from cigarettes. To date, no behavioral studies have examined whether secondary pipe or cigar smokers can be taught to smoke a moderate amount per day without inhaling. Even without inhalation, excessive consumption of pipe or cigar tobacco (four cigars or eight pipefuls daily) has been found to be associated with increased risk of disease and disability (Wynder & Hoffmann, 1972).

There is a controversy brewing over the recommended switch to low tar-low nicotine cigarettes as well. Recent evidence presented by Hammond, Garfinkle, Seidman, and Lew (1976) suggests that switching to these lower tar-lower nicotine smoking materials is accompanied by a lowering of death rates from lung cancer. Russell (1976) has suggested, however, that smokers should be encouraged to smoke low tar and moderately high nicotine brands so that they quickly receive a satisfying dose of nicotine, with a minimum of exposure to tars and carbon monoxide. One important point found in a number of controlled studies is that smokers adjust their patterns of inhalation and daily smoking consumption following a reduction in nicotine concentration in their cigarettes (Gritz & Jarvik, in press). Obviously, these plausible recommendations to reduce smoking risk require further justification and a firmer research foundation.

Evidence: Does It Work?

Except for the retrospective evidence of Hammond et al. (1976) cited earlier, there is no clear evidence that alterations in smoking habits or materials actually reduce risk. Methodological problems must be addressed in considering the available findings (Garfinkle, 1976). The problem of translating evidence based on associations in epidemiological research into therapeutic prescriptions is perhaps best illustrated by the finding that smokers make subtle adjustments in their habits when the nicotine content of cigarettes is reduced. Such compensating influences must be determined through careful prospective analyses. The literature in this area and the technological developments are too new to provide any clear answers.

Practicality: Will It Sell?

Even if safer methods for smoking can be found, there remains the question of whether the smoking public will accept the newer products. Certainly there has been widespread acceptance of filter tips and low tar-low nicotine brands—encouraged by the advertising campaigns that make explicit reference to the reduced risk of these brands and the lighter taste qualities.

Dramatic changes in product composition and design, however, might be expected to receive a more conservative response. Gori (1976) has acknowledged that some changes "alter the traditional flavor patterns [of cigarettes] and produce various degrees of conflicts with established standards of acceptance" (p. 1243). Consumer acceptance has yet to be tested although a recent brand has come on the market with extensive advertising that highlights its flavor enhancers requiring years to prepare. A new cigarette brand and related advertising campaigns have already attacked the artificial version with emphasis on return to a *natural* taste.

The Delicate Balance

Perhaps the key issue regarding less harmful methods of smoking involves the delicate balance between recommending substitute products and habits on the one hand and promoting complete cessation of the smoking habit on the other. Sensitive to this concern, the World Health Organization (1975) suggests that "the challenge is to present the approach to prevention without endangering the ultimate objective of persuading smokers to give up the habit" (p. 20). Even proponents of less hazardous cigarettes see merit to this challenge, and they argue, if somewhat ironically, that the newer products reduce the habit-forming features, so that smokers may find it easier to quit altogether (Gori, 1976). Of course smokers may, instead, switch to more traditional brands! Jarvik and Gritz (1977) have argued that the methods of reducing tars and other tobacco constituents would significantly lower the unpleasant effects of smoking, thereby depriving smokers of an immediate and salient incentive for quitting. Research and financial support should be focused on both targets: safer smoking and smoking cessation.

References

CHESSER, E. *Do you want to stop smoking?* New York: Cornerstone Library, 1963.

FREDERIKSEN, L. W. & PETERSON, G. L. Controlled smoking: Development and maintenance. *Addictive Behaviors,* 1976, *1*, 193–196.

GARFINKLE, L. Methodology for determining beneficial effect of less harmful cigarettes on lung cancer risk. In Wynder, E. L., Hoffman, D., & Gori, G. B. (eds.), *Proceedings of the 3rd World Conference on Smoking and Health: Modifying the risk for the smoker.* Washington, D.C., U.S. Government Printing Office, 1976, pp. 119–124. (DHEW No. NIH 76-1221).

GORI, G. B. Low-risk cigarettes: A prescription. *Science,* 1976, *194,* 1243–1246.

GRITZ, E. R. & JARVIK, M. E. Nicotine and smoking. In Iverson, L. L., Iverson, S. D. & Snyder, S. H. (eds.), *Handbook of psychopharmacology.* New York: Plenum Press, in press.

HAMMOND, E. C., GARFINKLE, L., SEIDMAN, H., & LEW, E. A. Some recent findings concerning cigarette smoking. *World Smoking & Health,* 1976, *1,* 41–44.

JARVIK, M. E. & GRITZ, E. R. Nicotine and tobacco. In Jarvik, M. E. (ed.), *Psychopharmacology in the practice of medicine.* New York: Appleton-Century-Crofts, 1977.

NATIONAL CANCER INSTITUTE. *Development of a flavor system for acceptability to smokers of candidate less hazardous cigarettes.* Bethesda, Md.: National Cancer Institute, 1976 (a).

NATIONAL CANCER INSTITUTE. *Smoking and health program.* Bethesda, Md.: National Cancer Institute, 1976 (b).

ROSS, W. S. Poison gases in your cigarettes. Part II: Hydrogen cyanide and nitrogen oxides. *Reader's Digest,* 1976, *109,* 92–98.

RUSSELL, M. A. H. Low-tar medium-nicotine cigarettes: A new approach to safer smoking. *British Medical Journal,* 1976, *1,* 1430–1433.

RUSSELL, M. A. H. Realistic goals for smoking and health: A case for safer smoking. *Lancet,* 1974, *1,* 254–258.

WORLD HEALTH ORGANIZATION, *Smoking and its effects on health.* Geneva: World Health Organization, 1975. (Technical Report Series 568).

WYNDER, E. L. & HOFFMANN, D Less harmful ways of smoking. *Journal of the National Cancer Institute*, 1972, *48*, 1749–1758.

WYNDER, E. L., MUSHINSKI, M. & STELLMAN, S. The epidemiology of the less harmful cigarette. In Wynder, E. L., Hoffmann, D., & Gori, G. B. (eds.), *Proceedings of the 3rd World Conference on Smoking and Health: Modifying the risk for the smoker.* Washington, D.C.: U.S. Government Printing Office, 1976, pp. 1–12. (DHEW No. NIH 76-1221).

THE ROLE OF DRUGS

Q: Are there drugs that will help me stop smoking?
A: There is no evidence that drugs promote smoking cessation. Some promising ideas deserve further attention, however.

Investigators have looked to drugs to help smokers discontinue the smoking habit. A basic assumption is that smoking is encouraged by a dependence on nicotine and the withdrawal effects that serve to discourage cessation. Treatment should provide some drug substitute for nicotine.

The substitute substance would presumably afford a temporary replacement or crutch, which would enable the individual to break old smoking patterns and establish a new repertoire of nonsmoking behaviors. Thus, more effective cessation programs might be aimed at breaking up established links while using a drug substitute.

Nicotine Replacement

The most obvious way to provide a smoking substitute is to use alternative sources of nicotine. Intravenous titration, that is, slowly feeding nicotine into a vein (Gritz & Jarvik, in press), has been an important laboratory method. But its use in more practical settings seems unlikely. By far the most attention has been focused on the use and evaluation of nicotine chewing gum (GUM) in smoking cessation activities.

Using a double-blind design, Russell, Wilson, Feyerabend, and Cole (1976) found that GUM had an inhibitory effect on smoking when participants were *not* trying to avoid normal smoking. GUM had no significant effect, however, when smokers made an effort to discontinue the smoking habit. Schneider, Popek, Jarvik, and Gritz (1977) reported three cases, in two of which GUM was prescribed ad libitum (as needed) as the primary smoking-control strategy. One smoker experienced considerable success with the treatment and was still abstinent seven months following treatment. The second smoker had more difficulty and resumed smoking three weeks after therapy terminated. Both individuals receiving GUM reported a marked reduction in dysphoria and craving, greater than was observed in the subject treated with a placebo gum. The authors suggested that gradual tapering in the use of the GUM might have improved the outcome in the unsuccessful case.

As these reports attest, the usefulness of GUM in smoking treatment looks promising, but it remains to be empirically validated. It is important to note that none of the studies reported in the literature has followed what was described earlier as the optimal design for using GUM, that is, to temporarily reduce the craving for smoking while the smoker is guided to break the ties between smoking and situations. More highly structured, packaged programs that include GUM should provide important evidence of its efficacy (Raw, 1976).

Three additional points: First, the effect of chewing nicotine gum may not be comparable to the effect achieved by smoking. The 4-mg variety appears to produce blood-nicotine concentrations comparable to or even greater than those obtained with normal smoking (Russell, Feyerabend & Cole, 1976, and Russell, Sutton, Feyerabend, Cole & Saloojee, 1977), but the bolus effect—successive concentrated doses—which follows the pattern of puffing and inhalation, is clearly quite different (Russell, 1976). Second, if it is ever made available to the community at large, GUM will probably have to be under tight prescription and supervision, because it could encourage more individuals to start using nicotine via chewing, especially young people, for whom chewing gum is an acceptable form of recreation (Hartelius & Tibbling, 1976). Third, prescriptions would be necessary because of the potential toxic side effects of ingesting GUM in quantity. Nicotine gum is currently not available by law although there are other legal ways of getting oral nicotine, including chewing tobacco and snuff.

Nicotine Mimics

The second major application of drug treatment to smoking has involved substances that are chemical and psychological mimics of nicotine. Mimics chemically resemble the original substance, thus possibly sharing its active properties. The major ingredient of many commercially available products for smoking cessation contains lobeline sulfate (Nicoban, Lobidan, Bantron, Tabusine, and others). The controlled research evidence for lobeline is very weak. Davison and Rosen (1972), for example, found it to be as ineffective as placebo compounds. These authors point out that there is no evidence that lobeline diminishes the intensity of smoking urges.

Another chemical compound called cytisine has witnessed extensive application in Europe as an aid to smoking cessation. The controlled research on cytisine is variable, and clinical case reports are difficult to interpret (Larson & Silvette, 1975).

Aversion Treatment?

One characteristic effect shared by all of the drugs that have been described is local irritation in the mouth and throat. The planned production of aversive events to help retard smoking has a long history, dating at least as far back as Fink's 1915 prescription for silver nitrate solution in the throat. Other substances, including quinine (Whitman, 1969), have been used but with relatively unimpressive results. It is critical, then, in evaluating the effects of GUM and other substitutes, to employ placebo compounds that produce irritation of similar magnitude.

Tranquilizers

Psychotropic antidepressive medication has been a familiar component in smoking cessation programs because it is presumed to help the smoker better cope with so-called withdrawal symptoms. Exact evaluation of tranquilizers in smoking control has not been conducted, probably because they have been used in conjunction with various other treatment prescriptions or strategies.

Summary

In conclusion, the usefulness of all pharmacological agents in smoking treatment must be considered unproven. There are some exciting possibilities for nicotine chewing gum, especially in conjunction with structured, guided practice in breaking established ties between smoking and situations. The role of tranquilizers is not clear, but the growing use of relaxation procedures in smoking treatment may signal a new vehicle for managing the stress associated with smoking withdrawal.

References

DAVISON, G. C. & ROSEN, R. C. Lobeline and reduction of cigarette smoking. *Psychological Reports*, 1972, *31*, 443–456.

FINK, B. *Tobacco.* New York: Abingdon Press, 1915.

GRITZ, E. R. & JARVIK, M. E. Nicotine and smoking. In Iverson, L. L., Iverson, S. D. & Snyder, S. H. (eds.), *Handbook of psychopharmacology*. New York: Plenum Press, in press.

HARTELIUS, J. & TIBBLING, L. Abuse and intoxication potential of nicotine chewing gum. *British Medical Journal*, 1976, 2, 812.

LARSON, P. S. & SILVETTE, H. *Tobacco: Experimental and clinical studies* (Supplement III). Baltimore: Williams & Wilkens, 1975.

RAW, M. Behavioral research in smoking withdrawal. *World Smoking and Health*, 1976, *1*, 4–7.

RUSSELL, M. A. H. Tobacco smoking and nicotine dependence. In Gibbons, R. J., Israel, Y., Kalent, H., Popham, R. E., Schmidt, W. & Smart, R. G. (eds.), *Research advances in alcohol and drug problems* (vol. 3). New York: Wiley, 1976, pp. 1–47.

RUSSELL, M. A. H., FEYERABEND, C. & COLE, P. V. Plasma nicotine levels after cigarette smoking and chewing nicotine gum. *British Medical Journal*, 1976, *1*, 1043–1046.

RUSSELL, M. A. H., SUTTON, S. R., FEYERABEND, C., COLE, P. V. & SALOOJEE, Y. Nicotine chewing gum as a substitute for smoking. *British Medical Journal*, 1977, *1*, 1060–1063.

RUSSELL, M. A. H., WILSON, C., FEYERABEND, C. & COLE, P. V. Effect of nicotine chewing gum as an aid to cigarette withdrawal. *British Medical Journal*, 1976, 2, 391–393.

SCHNEIDER, N. G., POPEK, P., JARVIK, M. E. & GRITZ, E R. Nicotine gum and smoking cessation. *American Journal of Psychiatry*, 1977, *134*, 439–440.

WHITMAN, T. L. Modification of chronic smoking behavior: A comparison of three approaches. *Behavior Research and Therapy*, 1969, 7, 257–263.

RISKS OF SMOKING
IN PREGNANCY

Q: Is smoking more dangerous during pregnancy?
A: Yes, smoking beyond the first trimester is related to increased risks of unsuccessful pregnancy.

Smoking during pregnancy increases the likelihood of a number of complications. Smoking has been found to be related to reduction in infant birth weights. Smokers' infants tend to be small for their gestational age, suggesting some form of direct retardation of fetal growth. The mechanisms underlying this observation have not been firmly established, but the available evidence suggests that toxic components are transmitted to the fetus, that the fetus's vitamin metabolism is disturbed, and that available oxygen is reduced (DHEW, 1973). There is a dose-response relationship: Women who smoke more cigarettes each day have a higher risk of low-birth-weight infants than women who smoke fewer cigarettes daily.

There is a similar dose-response relationship between smoking during pregnancy and perinatal death, death in the period shortly before or after birth. Some of the epidemiological evidence points to a relationship between smoking and spontaneous abortion, while much stronger evidence shows a link to stillbirth, particularly in women who have a past or present history of obstetrical complications (DHEW, 1973). The magnitude of risk has been estimated, and the percentages suggest that more than 4,600 perinatal deaths in this country (DHEW, 1973) and 1,500 perinatal deaths in Great Britain (Goldstein, 1977) can be attributed to smoking among pregnant women.

Even following the infant's birth, it is exposed to dangers related to parental smoking. In one recent study, for example, secondhand smoke around the home was found to be related to crib death (Bergman & Wiesner, 1976). Other studies (Colley, Holland, & Corkhill, 1974, and Lebowitz & Burrows, 1976) have found an increased incidence of respiratory problems in children exposed to parental smoking.

Remedies for the Problem

Fortunately, the epidemiological research literature suggests that expectant women who are able to completely stop smoking prior to their fourth month of pregnancy (in their first trimester) completely eliminate the excess risk of infant mortality (Butler, Goldstein, & Ross, 1972). Quitting after the fourth month would presumably still reduce risk, but the extent of that reduction has not been determined. Although controlled prospective clinical trials are required to firmly establish the benefits derived from quitting smoking in the first trimester (Barker & Rose, 1976), the available evidence clearly points to the preventive benefits of not smoking during pregnancy.

A number of recommendations stem from this evidence on excess risks for pregnant women. A recent report by the American Cancer Society (ACS, 1976), for example, has suggested that all expectant women should receive counseling about stopping smoking during their first prenatal visit. An even more definite recommendation is that smoking counseling should begin *before* pregnancy as a routine part of annual exams along with the Pap smear test. Proposals for a national health plan have included provisions for counseling pregnant women about the risks of smoking as well as instruction in effective management procedures (*Preventive Medicine, USA*, 1976, p. 49).

Recent medical textbooks in obstetrics have proposed that physicians play a more active role in suggesting that their patients stop all smoking during pregnancy (Held,

1977; Macgillivray & Campbell, 1976). Routine suggestions of this type would be a considerable improvement over current practice, but for many women this admonition may not be sufficient to get them to stop smoking. Training in nonsmoking skills may be required as well.

In a recent proposal for research and development of skills-training programs for pregnant women smokers, Danaher (1977) suggested that existing behavioral smoking-control strategies could be adapted to fit the treatment needs of this special population at risk. These treatment protocols could be supplemented with educational materials describing the excess risks associated with smoking during pregnancy. The short-term goal of such programs would be to assist women to stop smoking prior to the second trimester and for the duration of their pregnancies. This immediate goal could subsequently be broadened to encourage the maintenance of nonsmoking once the child is born by stressing the continuing risks to children growing up in a smoke-filled home environment. To date, only a few programs of this type have emerged (Danaher, 1977).

Smoking-control activities for expectant women smokers might provide important benefits by decreasing the risk of infant mortality and by encouraging permanent cessation by parents, who, in turn, reduce their susceptibility to chronic disease. Finally, the child raised in a nonsmoking family environment might not be so tempted to begin smoking later in life.

More research is clearly needed. Additional epidemiological investigations would help pinpoint the risks both at birth and later in development. Controlled tests of treatment packages, combining skills training and educational materials, would establish effective long-term aids for smoking cessation. Professional education and corresponding changes in medical practice would increase women's awareness of the risks of smoking throughout pregnancy and would encourage enduring behavior change. The skyrocketing number of smokers among women of childbearing age in this country serves to underscore the critical needs in this area.

References

AMERICAN CANCER SOCIETY. *Task force on tobacco and cancer: Target 5.* New York: American Cancer Society, 1976.

BARKER, D. J. P., & ROSE, G. *Epidemiology in medical practice.* New York: Churchill Livingstone, 1976.

BERGMAN, A. B., & WIESNER, L. A. Relationship of passive cigarette-smoking to sudden infant death syndrome. *Pediatrics,* 1976, *58,* 665–668.

BUTLER, N. R., GOLDSTEIN, H., & ROSS, E. M. Cigarette smoking in pregnancy: The influence on birth weight and perinatal mortality. *British Medical Journal,* 1972, *2,* 127–130.

COLLEY, J. R. T., HOLLAND, W. W., & CORKHILL, R. T. Influence of passive smoking and parental phlegm on pneumonia and bronchitis in early childhood. *Lancet,* 1974, *2,* 1031.

DANAHER, B. G. Smoking in pregnant women: Consequences and their prevention. Testimony presented to the National Commission on Smoking and Public Policy. Los Angeles, March 1977.

DEPARTMENT OF HEALTH, EDUCATION, AND WELFARE. *The health consequences of smoking* (DHEW Publication HSM 73-8704). Washington, D. C.: U. S. Government Printing Office, 1973.

GOLDSTEIN, H. Smoking in pregnancy: Some notes on the statistical controversy. *British Journal of Preventive and Social Medicine,* 1977, *31,* 13–17.

HELD, B. Antepartum care. In Conn, H. F. (ed.), *Current therapy, 1977.* Philadelphia: Saunders, 1977, pp. 800–808.

LEBOWITZ, M. D., & BURROWS, B. Respiratory symptoms related to smoking habits of family adults. *Chest,* 1976, *1,* 48–50.

MACGILLIVRAY, I., & CAMPBELL, D. M. A prospective study of factors affecting intrauterine growth (with an emphasis on blood pressure and diuretics). In Lindheimer, M. D., Katz, A. I., & Zuspan, F. P. (eds.), *Hypertension in pregnancy.* New York: Wiley, 1976.

Preventive medicine USA: Theory, practice and application of prevention in personal health services. New York: Prodist, 1976.

SMOKING AND WEIGHT GAIN

Q: Do people always gain weight once they stop smoking, and is this caused by some changes in the body?

A: Not all smokers gain weight when they try to stop smoking. But enough smokers experience weight problems or worry about it that it is a major concern. Changes in eating behavior rather than metabolic changes in the body may be an explanation.

In a recent nationwide survey, almost 55 percent of American adults reported that fears about gaining weight kept many smokers from making serious efforts to stop smoking (United States Public Health Service, 1976). Since many people assume that weight and smoking are inversely related—when one is reduced, the other increases—it is quite likely that weight gain is an important factor in motivating ex-smokers to resume the smoking habit.

The notorious link between smoking and body weight has received so much discussion that it has become part of the shared folklore of smoking. In turning to the medical-research literature for evidence that might support widespread beliefs, it quickly becomes clear that very little careful evaluation of this important relationship has occurred.

Research Findings

The sparse literature available appears to support the conclusion that ex-smokers gain weight when they stop smoking. The magnitude of weight gain is about 5 kg or 10 pounds (Brozek & Keys, 1957; Comstock & Stone, 1972; Lincoln, 1969; and Shephard, Rode & Ross, 1973). With one exception (Shephard et al., 1973), these studies have not looked at weight changes among participants in smoking-control programs but instead have focused on individuals who stopped smoking on their own. Moreover, these studies have focused almost exclusively on men; Shephard et al. (1973) found that women gained more weight following cessation than did male participants. At least one study (Comstock & Stone, 1972) found a dose-response relationship between smoking and weight gain: The greater the reduction in smoking, the more pronounced the weight increase observed.

Very little has been established about the possible underlying mechanisms that might explain weight gain following cessation of smoking. An early hypothesis forwarded by Brozek and Keys (1957) argued that smoking depressed the experience of hunger. There is some evidence that smoking cigarettes can become a means for controlling excessive eating. Morganstern (1974) described a case in which a nonsmoker successfully used cigarette smoke as a noxious stimulus to avoid overeating and lose 41 pounds. Smoking cigarettes as a weight-control tactic can presumably continue long after the smoker becomes accustomed to the smoke. To date, no studies have attempted to measure changes in eating behaviors in individuals who stop smoking.

A behavioral hypothesis that emerges from many clinical observations is that ex-smokers are prone to overeating because they use food as a substitute for smoking or because they find food more attractive with increased sensitivity to food aroma and taste. A competing hypothesis, one more favored by medical researchers, is that smoking cessation causes a change in body metabolism so that the same amount of eating produces an increase in weight. In the only direct empirical test of this hypothesis, Glauser, Glauser, Reidenberg, Rusy, and Tallarida (1970) found a diminished basal-oxygen consumption in six of seven smokers shortly after they stopped smoking. These authors contend that the metabolic change they found would produce weight gain unless changes occurred in caloric intake or physical activity. Lincoln (1969) presents some corroborating evidence in his report, to the effect that ex-smokers have to cut back increasingly larger caloric intake in order to maintain their weight. Interestingly, by one year after quitting, the weight and calorie balance is approximately the same for ex-smokers and individuals who never smoked, a similar point having been made in the research of Khosla and Lowe (1971).

Pragmatic Perspective

No matter what underlying mechanisms may be found to explain the relationship between smoking and body weight, careful balancing of caloric intake and exercise enables most ex-smokers to successfully manage their weight. Programs for smoking cessation should include information about diet and exercise. If special weight problems are encountered, then changes in eating behaviors are needed, perhaps directed by authoritative guides in weight control (Jeffrey & Katz, 1977; Mahoney & Mahoney, 1976; Stuart & Davis, 1972). The health risk of a few temporary extra pounds is negligible when compared to the risks of smoking.

References

BROZEK, J. & KEYS, A. Changes of body weight in normal men who stop smoking cigarettes. *Science*, 1957, *125*, 1203.

COMSTOCK, G. W. & STONE, R. W. Changes in body weight and subcutaneous fatness related to smoking habits. *Archives of Environmental Health*, 1972, *24*, 271–276.

GLAUSER, S. C., GLAUSER, E. M., REIDENBERG, M. M., RUSY, B. F. & TALLARIDA, R. J. Metabolic changes associated with the cessation of smoking. *Archives of Environmental Health*, 1970, *20*, 377–381.

JEFFREY, D. B. & KATZ, R. *Take it off and keep it off: A behavioral program for weight loss and healthy living.* Englewood Cliffs, N. J.: Prentice-Hall, 1977.

KHOSLA, T. & LOWE, C. R. Obesity and smoking habits. *British Medical Journal*, 1971, *4*, 10–13.

LINCOLN, J. E. Weight gain after cessation of smoking. *Journal of the American Medical Association*, 1969, *210*, 1765.

MAHONEY, M. J. & MAHONEY, K. *Permanent weight control.* New York: Norton, 1976.

MORGANSTERN, K. P. Cigarette smoke as a noxious stimulus in self-managed aversion therapy for compulsive eating: Technique and case illustration. *Behavior Therapy*, 1974, *5*, 255–260.

SHEPHARD, R. J., RODE, A. & ROSS, R. Reinforcement of a smoking withdrawal program: The role of the physiologist and the psychologist. *Canadian Journal of Public Health*, 1973, *64*, 542–551.

STUART, R. B. & DAVIS, B. *Slim chance in a fat world.* Champaign, Ill.: Research Press, 1972.

UNITED STATES PUBLIC HEALTH SERVICE. *Adult use of tobacco, 1975.* Atlanta: Center for Disease Control, 1976.

appendix B

New Arenas for Smoking Control

PRIMARY PREVENTION OF SMOKING IN SCHOOLS

Epidemiologic research on cardiovascular disease suggests that increasing effort should be devoted to primary prevention: persuading young people not to adopt the smoking habit (Blackburn, 1974; Kannel & Dawber, 1972). Some reviewers have gone so far as to call cardiovascular disease a *pediatric* problem! By most accounts, unfortunately, smoking among young persons—particularly young women—appears to be increasing in recent years (American Cancer Society, 1976 and Department of Health, Education, and Welfare, 1974).

Because of the efficiency of reaching many young people in a learning setting, several important efforts have been made to develop new school health curricula that would promote avoidance of smoking. For the most part, these well-intentioned health-education programs have relied on transmitting the risks of chronic smoking, most of which are long-term consequences, and these programs have failed to have any marked influence on discouraging adoption of the smoking habit (Jeffreys, 1961). Recent research in the development of novel health curricula aimed at primary prevention of smoking and cardiovascular disease appears promising.

Earlier evidence from large surveys indicated that various patterns are associated with the early adoption of cigarette smoking (Bynner, 1970). For example, parental and peer smoking are strongly related to adoption, as is the desire for a young person to appear more adult or be rebellious (see Table 1 in Chapter 1). These patterns provide possible clues about the most effective targets for prevention.

Focusing on the peer-pressure influences on the early adoption of smoking, two innovative programs have developed structured learning experiences that are aimed at better equipping young people to resist social influences. A key point is that this is accomplished without the young person losing any semblance of personal dignity. Both programs are partly based on inoculation-counter argument theory which suggests that forewarning about social pressures can lead to more effective resistance to those pressures (McGuire, 1969).

Evans (1976) has employed videotaped vignettes that illustrate key points of peer pressures for cigarette adoption. These videotapes are shown in classrooms and followed by directed discussion about peer pressures and related coping strategies. While the risks of smoking are mentioned, the innovative aspect of Evans's materials is their attempt to model both the pressures for early adoption and also the successful behavioral responses enabling a young person to resist those pressures.

McAlister (1976) has reported preliminary work using a peer-led discussion format in junior high schools that emphasizes (a) outlining the risks and benefits of smoking, (b) public commitment to avoid smoking, (c) practice of coping skills through role playing to resist pressures to smoke and maintain personal dignity, and (d) follow-up contact. Mediated materials (videotape, for example) will be developed once the preliminary intervention packages have been formalized.

Data on the efficacy of these more innovative programs are currently being collected. Validation of young persons' self-reported smoking or nonsmoking will be critical for this evaluation. Many research issues remain: how more efficient mediated materials, such as videotape, can be effectively used; whether peers are effective discussion leaders; which are the critical times for intervention and whether certain grade levels are more critical intervention times than others; and how to improve methods for controlled clinical trials of the intervention package. It is likely that considerable effort and money will be spent in primary prevention programs for the schools in the near future. Controlled empirical evaluations are already planned or under way. Programs that attempt to include behavioral-skills training may provide a more realistic hope for behavior change than the more traditional sharing of risk-benefit information about the dangers of chronic smoking.

References

AMERICAN CANCER SOCIETY. *Summary of findings: Study about cigarette smoking among teenage girls and young women,* 1976.

BLACKBURN, H. Progress in the epidemiology and prevention of coronary heart disease. In Yu, P. N. and Goodwin, J. F. (eds.), *Progress in cardiology* (vol. 3). Philadelphia: Lea & Febiger, 1974, pp. 1–36.

BYNNER, J. M. Behavioral research into children's smoking: Some implications for anti-smoking strategy. *Royal Society of Health Journal*, 1970, *90*, 159–163.

DEPARTMENT OF HEALTH, EDUCATION, AND WELFARE. *Patterns and prevalence of teenage cigarette smoking: 1968, 1970, 1972, 1974.* DHEW Publication (HSM) 74–8701, 1974.

EVANS, R. I. Smoking in children: Developing a social psychological strategy of deterrence. *Preventive Medicine*, 1976, *5*, 122–127.

JEFFREYS, M. Catch them before they start: A report on an attempt to influence children's smoking habits. *Health Education Journal*, 1961, *19*, 3–17.

KANNEL, W. B. & DAWBER, T. R. Atherosclerosis as a pediatric problem. *Journal of Pediatrics*, 1972, *80*, 544.

MCALISTER, A. Preventing and stopping cigarette smoking: Some problems and techniques. In Thoresen, C. E. (ch.), Behavioral self-control with children and adolescents. Symposium presented at the annual meeting of the American Educational Research Association, San Francisco, 1976.

MCGUIRE, W. J. The nature of attitudes and attitude change. In Lindzey, G. & Aronson, E. (eds.), *Handbook of Social Psychology* (vol. 3). Reading, Mass.: Addison-Wesley, 1969, pp. 136–314.

OCCUPATIONAL SMOKING-CONTROL PROGRAMS

Smoking-control efforts have only recently begun to emerge within the business community. The impetus behind this evolving trend can be traced to a number of related factors. Many businesses are concerned about maintaining the health of their cadre of executives and their work force. After investing thousands of dollars in training an executive, for example, it is an obvious waste of money to allow smoking to subtract years of his or her productive involvement in the organization. Similarly, the active work force might be maintained and absenteeism reduced if more healthful life-styles are promoted, including the reduction of cigarette smoking, estimated to be responsible for 77 million lost workdays annually (Terry, 1971). The skyrocketing costs of health-insurance coverage also point to the need to promote preventive health programs among which smoking cessation would be a prominent member. Finally, recent court decisions (Shimp, Blumrosen & Finifter, 1976) place the responsibility for providing healthy working environments on businesses.

There are also special reasons that would predispose certain businesses to become involved in smoking cessation activities. For example, those sectors that have the highest incidence of smoking among their work forces would have a more salient need (Sterling & Weinkam, 1976). Environments that present risks to workers that are compounded, or acted upon synergistically, by habitual smoking (such as asbestos manufacturing) would also be prime centers for smoking programs (Hoffmann & Wynder, 1976).

McAbee (1968) described the warm reception smoking control programs received among the employees and executives in a telephone company. He also commented that groups could not be arbitrarily composed, because programs attempting to mix employees and executives would simply not survive in the hierarchy of business communities. While preventive health and smoking-control programs are currently under way in enlightened small businesses, there are optimistic signs that larger industries are developing a sensitivity to promoting smoking-cessation programs. For example, the Ford Motor Company, Dearborn, Mich., provides opportunities for smoking cessation as a part of its comprehensive heart attack risk reduction program.

Treatment programs in business can take the form of supplying information and giving admonitions about smoking during annual company-sponsored physical examinations. In the only available evaluation of this level of intervention, Pincherle and Wright (1970) found that only 13 percent of businessmen gave up smoking entirely, while, much to the investigators' dismay, 7 percent adopted the habit or increased their smoking!

More intensive intervention was evaluated by Meyer and Henderson (1974). They selected men from an electronics-research firm who had been diagnosed as being at high risk of cardiovascular disease in preliminary physical examinations. During a physical exam, each participant was told by a doctor to modify the risk behaviors, including smoking, that were detected. Two-thirds of the participants were then assigned to either an intensive treatment group exposed to 36 hours of professional contact, with a focus on all risk behaviors, including smoking, overeating, and lack of exercise, *or* to a condition in which each participant met individually with a trained health educator for information and support in regard to risk behaviors. At the three-month follow-up, there were no significant differences between the intensive condition (10 percent abstinent), the information condition (11 percent abstinent) or the physician-consultation condition (17 percent abstinent).

The goal for business interventions is to develop a cost-effective treatment package that can reach a maximum number of employees. Options within the program for group and paired interactions might be helpful. And traditional approaches to behavioral control of smoking might have to be modified somewhat to fit the setting and the population.

One exciting and novel approach to smoking control takes advantage of the salary-bonus options available to an employer. Profit can be used to help motivate the exploration and then the eventual adoption of new life-styles by working individuals. Rosen and Lichtenstein (1977), for example, found that the owner of a small ambulance service was able to reduce smoking on the job by providing financial bonuses for successful behavior changes. Whether on-the-job behavior changes translate into overall behavioral changes has not yet been determined.

The considerable potential for business-oriented smoking cessation programs and activities has only recently been explored, and a host of intriguing questions can be asked. Will health enhancement be most effective if it involves some financial incentives, or are praise and attention from superiors in an organization just as effective? Will modeling from superiors who continue smoking discourage participation or reduce effectiveness? Careful evaluation of each intervention is important to development of our knowledge and experience in occupational-smoking interventions. It is expected that greater advances will be made in this arena because occupational smoking-control programs represent both sound financial and health priorities.

References

HOFFMANN, D., & WYNDER, E. L. Smoking and occupational cancers. *Preventive Medicine*, 1976, *5*, 245–261.

MCABEE, N. K. Adult decision making: Programs in occupational settings. In *National conference on smoking and health: A summary of proceedings.* New York: National Interagency Council on Smoking and Health, 1967.

MEYER, A. J., & HENDERSON, J. B. Multiple risk factor reduction in the prevention of cardiovascular disease. *Preventive Medicine*, 1974, *3*, 225–236.

PINCHERLE, G., & WRIGHT, H. B. Smoking habits of business

executives: Doctor variation in reducing cigarette consumption. *The Practitioner,* 1970, *205*, 209–212.

ROSEN, G. M., & LICHTENSTEIN, E. A worker's incentive program for the reduction of cigarette smoking. *Journal of Consulting and Clinical Psychology,* 1977, *45*, 957.

SHIMP, D. M., BLUMROSEN, A. W., & FINIFTER, S. B. *How to protect your health at work.* Salem, N. J.: Environmental Improvement Associates, 1976 (available through National Interagency Council on Smoking and Health).

STERLING, T. D., & WEINKAM, J. J. Smoking characteristics by type of employment. *Journal of Occupational Medicine,* 1976, *18*, 743–754.

TERRY, L. The future of an illusion. *American Journal of Public Health,* 1971, *61*, 233–240.

GROWING ROLE OF
THE HEALTH-CARE COMMUNITY

Physicians and other health-care professionals are coming to realize the necessity of encouraging changes in patients' lifestyles in order to reduce present illness and prevent the onset of disease. Unfortunately, those health professionals who acknowledge the need for behavioral changes are often untrained or have no time necessary for effective intervention.

Practical, efficient treatment protocols that would enable the active health-care professional to aid patients in their efforts to discontinue smoking are in great need. In their recent comprehensive review of the role of the physician in smoking cessation, Lichtenstein & Danaher (in press) outlined some basic strategies for the effective office management of cigarette smoking. The procedures presented in this present book are well suited to this purpose, too, because their self-help format would presumably reduce the time required of the health professional while still providing the structured cessation program.

Health professionals can make key contributions to smoking cessation on a number of levels. They can stop smoking themselves—and have done so with considerable success—so that they present a powerful model of nonsmoking. They can also provide smoking-and-health information in the physical environment of their offices, in the waiting room area, for example, which increases the general interest in and enthusiasm for nonsmoking. Health professionals can assume a more active role and admonish patients to stop smoking. Even more active help could take the form of directed referral of the smoker to an effective treatment agency. Finally, the health professional could expand traditional horizons by very actively prescribing cessation strategies with the attendant follow-up over the course of treatment.

The research evidence on the therapeutic impact of physicians' office management of smoking in medical settings has been summarized by Lichtenstein and Danaher (in press). The most impressive changes in smoking behavior often followed diagnosis or firsthand experience with some serious condition, for example, cardiovascular disease leading to myocardial infarction. Extended contact with a physician appears to have facilitated the most enduring changes in smoking behavior. Less impressive levels of abstinence were found when physicians routinely made suggestions about smoking cessation to patients who were not suffering from any smoking-related disease and who had expressed no particular interest in quitting.

The foregoing discussion of the physician should not obscure the fact that many other health-care professionals can provide helpful assistance. The list of potential providers or practitioners of health services could include the physician-extender (office staff members, health educators, nurse practitioners, physicians' assistants), dentists (Seffrin & Stauffer, 1976), pharmacists, nurses, and others.

The diversity of input sources and points for intervention is displayed in Figure 14. The three-dimensional prevention matrix identifies service providers and their activities. (The list is not exhaustive and would appropriately include behavioral scientists.) Health service providers would describe the rationale for suggested changes (health education), outline methods for self-change (health promotion), and provide care once disease is first identified (early diagnosis and treatment). It is important to note that the targets for intervention need not be limited to patients; they can be expanded to include family members and other groups in the community. The multifaceted approach along various avenues of health-care delivery has many advantages, the chief of which may be that a more pervasive theme of nonsmoking could encourage personal initiative to stop smoking and help support nonsmoking over time.

Several promising signs point to a broadening approach to the prevention of disease through smoking-cessation activities within the health-care community. First, multidisciplinary clinical research teams are turning to behavioral science for more effective interventions (Farquhar, Maccoby, Wood, et. al., 1977). Second, a new subspecialty called behavioral medicine has emerged and has already made significant contributions to health care based on applications of behavioral psychology (Katz & Zlutnik, 1975 and Rachman & Philips, 1975). Finally, funding agencies have gone on record as recognizing the important role of behavioral science in plans for improving national health care (United States Public Health Service, 1976).

Concerted efforts within the health-care community should have an impact on individual smokers, recent ex-smokers, and individuals who might otherwise have initiated the tobacco habit. They may also yield an even more effective technology for long-lasting smoking cessation.

Figure 14
The Prevention Matrix

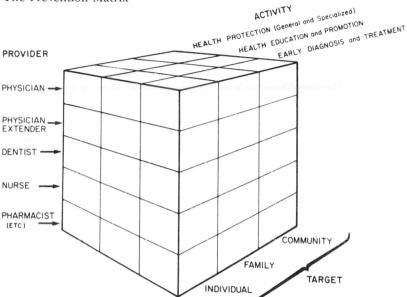

Reprinted with permission from *Preventive Medicine USA: Education and Training of Health Manpower for Prevention.* New York: Prodist, 1976.

References

FARQUHAR, J. W., MACCOBY, N., WOOD, P. D., ALEXANDER, J. K., BRIETROSE, H., BROWN, B. W., HASKELL, W. L., McALISTER, A. L., MEYER, A. J., NASH, J. D., & STERN, M. P. Community education for cardiovascular health. *Lancet*, 1977, *1*, 1192–1195.

KATZ, R. G., & ZLUTNIK, S. (eds.), *Behavior therapy and health care: Principles and applications.* New York: Pergamon, 1975.

LICHTENSTEIN, E., & DANAHER, B. G. Role of the physician in smoking cessation. In Brashear, R. E., & Rhodes, M. L. (eds.). *Chronic obstructive lung disease: Clinical treatment and management.* St. Louis: Mosby, in press.

Preventive medicine USA: Education and training of health manpower for prevention. New York: Prodist, 1976.

RACHMAN, S. J., & PHILIPS, C. *Psychology and medicine.* London: Temple Smith, 1975.

SEFFRIN, J. R., & STAUFFER, B. J. Patient education on cigarette smoking: The dentist's role. *Journal of the American Dental Association,* 1976, *92,* 751-754.

UNITED STATES PUBLIC HEALTH SERVICE, *Forward plan for health, FY 1977-1981* (DHEW Publication OS-76-50024). Washington, D. C.: U. S. Government Printing Office, 1975.

LEGISLATIVE MEASURES

It must be brought home to legislators that while it is up to the individual to decide to stop smoking, the legislature has the responsibility of enacting measures that will encourage him to do so.

(World Health Organization, 1975, p. 80)

Because the probability of prohibiting all smoking seems remote, it is important to consider less comprehensive restrictions. Patterns of smoking behavior are sensitive to the influences of legislative measures. Most authorities argue that law cannot be the sole method of smoking control because education must also be included. Moreover, legal measures cannot be expected to work in a vacuum. Instead, they must be used in a manner that corresponds at least partly to the prevailing public sentiment regarding smoking and health. This discussion will focus on specific examples of legislative measures, including the following: (1) taxation, (2) advertising restrictions, and (3) smoking-area restrictions.

Taxation

Additional costs can be applied to any product to discourage its consumption. Unfortunately, taxation often provides insufficient deterrence, and at the same time it can provide governments with considerable additional revenue. That is also unfortunate in the sense that as revenues accumulate from this source of taxation—more than $2 billion were spent on tobacco products in 1975—public-health goals may be overshadowed by the profit motive. Widespread cessation would quite clearly result in marked reductions in tax revenues.

Taxation in some form is currently applied to cigarettes and other tobacco products in all 50 states and the District of Columbia. In 1976, these taxes ranged from 2 to 21 cents per pack (U.S. Department of Agriculture, 1977). While critics have argued that this arrangement has resulted in more costs than benefits (Herron, 1968), taxes on tobacco products are nonetheless considered rather commonplace. Russell (1973) found that cigarette consumption by British men varied systematically with price changes over a 25-year period. Across-the-board taxation can also be amended to encourage less hazardous smoking. In several cities, and at different times, taxes are scaled according to tar and nicotine levels per brand: The higher the tars and nicotine, the higher the taxes. Federal legislation is currently being considered for similar differential taxation. Complicating this approach is the contention of some experts that safer cigarettes should be moderately high in nicotine but low in tars so that smokers can get their nicotine with fewer cigarettes (Russell, 1974).

The revenues generated from cigarette taxation can also be a potential gold mine for antismoking efforts. Educational and advertising campaigns encouraging nonsmoking and providing specific cessation methods could be funded from such tax revenues. Moreover, needed research into more effective cessation methods could be supported from such money. To date, this sort of enlightened use of tax revenues has not been realized. But tobacco taxation is currently in effect in most states and in many countries around the world.

Advertising Restrictions

Most of us can remember seeing advertisements for tobacco products on TV. However, in 1971 Congress banned all advertising messages over electronic media. This restrictive legislation represents one example of the power of legal constraints on smoking. This and many other measures have been documented and analyzed in an excellent treatise on the subject by Fritschler (1975). The historical pattern of a public-health thrust and a tobacco-industry counterthrust was suddenly altered in the early 1960's as the Federal Trade Commission, supported by documentation from the 1964 Surgeon General's Report, assumed a more stalwart enforcement role in bureaucratic politics. More recent restrictions have included the elimination of little-cigar advertising from the electronic media and the mandatory "clear and conspicuous" health warning on all cigarette advertisements ("Warning: The Surgeon General Has Determined That Cigarette Smoking Is Dangerous to Your Health").

Unfortunately, these legislative restrictions have not produced any overall reduction in public smoking. In fact, the tobacco industry has realized an estimated 30 percent savings in advertising costs, since the electronic media ban went into effect, while the sales of cigarettes have actually increased! When tobacco products were banned, the anti-smoking messages receiving equal media time were similarly excised. Thus well-meaning changes for public health have actually served to shift the immense advertising budgets for tobacco into other channels. O'Connor (1976) reports that the top 20 brands had an advertising budget of over \$234 million in 1975. More advertising than ever is appearing in magazines, in newspapers, and on billboards.

The health warnings on package and advertising labels present an interesting case in point. Labeling that describes the health hazards of smoking was required by the FTC when it became impossible to adjudicate the health implications and subtleties in advertising. In his thorough review of this issue, Whiteside (1974) has argued that these labels have been at least as helpful to the tobacco industry as they have been effective warnings to smokers. He cites the fact that prior to the addition of these warnings, editors of newspapers and magazines were becoming somewhat reluctant to continue cigarette advertising. In fact, *The New York Times* in 1970 required a warning on the part of tobacco producers if the ads were to appear in the newspaper. The tobacco producers refused and withdrew all their ads in response. With the advent of the FTC health label, however, the producers were free to submit ads again, and in 1973 the *Times* ran 264,000 lines of cigarette advertising! The warning message further protected the tobacco industry because it diminished responsibility for the health consequences of smoking and thus decreased the likelihood that courts would hold the manufacturers legally liable for the effects of smoking on individuals.

Changes have been suggested in the label itself to strengthen its impact. The American Cancer Society has suggested that it should be changed to read "Cigarette Smoking Is Hazardous to Your Health and May Cause Death" (Business Week, 1975). Foreign governments are also exploring such changes, and Sweden is planning to institute a "menu" of warnings for cigarette advertising (see Figure 15). It is interesting to note that the messages on Sweden's labels attempt to pinpoint specific types of risk—cancer and cardiovascular disease, for example—and populations at risk

Figure 15
Warning Notices to Be Carried
on Cigarette Packages in Sweden

THE PERSON WHO STOPS SMOKING WILL SOON BE MORE FIT *National Board of Health and Welfare*	**SMOKER'S COUGH IN THE MORNING?** Smoker's cough is a sign of early ill-health. The cough will cease if you stop smoking. *National Board of Health and Welfare*
THE MORE YOU SMOKE THE GREATER HEALTH RISKS WILL THERE BE *National Board of Health and Welfare*	**SMOKING DAMAGES THE LUNGS!** It begins with a smoker's cough and it may end up with lung cancer or other lung diseases. *National Board of Health and Welfare*
ASBESTOS is especially dangerous to smokers. If you work in an environment with such pollution you should stop smoking. *National Board of Health and Welfare*	**THE PERSON WHO STOPS SMOKING INCREASES HIS CHANCES OF REMAINING HEALTHY.** *National Board of Health and Welfare*
YOU WHO HAVE BEEN SMOKING FOR A LONG TIME! It has been proved that those who stop smoking will decrease the health risks. *National Board of Health and Welfare*	**SMOKERS HAVE MORE SICKNESS THAN NON-SMOKERS** *National Board of Health and Welfare*
WHICH CIGARETTES ARE MOST DANGEROUS? Those yielding most carbon monoxide, tar and nicotine. But it also depends HOW you smoke. *National Board of Health and Welfare*	**YOU WHO HAVE BEEN SMOKING FOR A LONG TIME!** Stopping smoking is useful — the risk for disease will decrease and your fitness will improve. *National Board of Health and Welfare*
DISEASES OF THE HEART AND ARTERIES Smokers run an increased risk of heart attacks and certain diseases of the arteries. *National Board of Health and Welfare*	**IF YOU STILL MUST SMOKE** Avoid inhaling and leave long butts and you will absorb less of dangerous substances. *National Board of Health and Welfare*
NON-SMOKERS HAVE LONGER AVERAGE LIFE THAN SMOKERS *National Board of Health and Welfare*	**SMOKING AND AIR POLLUTION** is a bad combination. Smokers are more sensitive to air pollution. *National Board of Health and Welfare*
SMOKING DURING PREGNANCY MAY HARM THE CHILD *National Board of Health and Welfare*	**YOU WHO ARE YOUNG!** The earlier you begin smoking the more seriously your health will be affected. *National Board of Health and Welfare*

Reprinted with permission from L. M. Ramstrom, New ideas in Sweden's tobacco labeling Act in *World Smoking & Health*, 1976, *1*, pp. 28–31.

(young smokers, workers, and pregnant women). Whiteside (1974) has also made the very appropriate suggestion that a warning label should constitute about 20 percent of the total area devoted to an ad, whatever its size. Moreover, he has suggested that warnings should be appropriate to the advertisement's audience. For example, cigarette ads in women's magazines should include a warning about the effects of smoking on fetal development and unsuccessful pregnancy. Finally, there have been many suggestions that the labels should list some of the presumed ways of smoking in a less hazardous manner.

Designated Smoking Areas

As never before, the last few years have witnessed a growing physical separation of smoking from nonsmoking. The impetus for this activity, or, perhaps more accurately, the validation for it, has arisen from the research evidence showing risks of secondhand, or passive, smoking for a nonsmoker, especially if the nonsmoker has any cardiorespiratory disease. Public transportation and public buildings have been the early targets for restrictions of smoking. At first, the tobacco industry adopted a rather low profile in response to this movement. More recently, however, it has hired advertising and public relations help to mount a counter campaign emphasizing the rights of smokers (Stencel, 1977). It seems likely that controversy over such issues will continue.

Penalties have been levied as well: there have been reports from a major city that dozens of smokers have been jailed after they were unable to post a $25 bond for violating smoking restrictions on city buses and trains. Of course, not all of this progress has been made as the direct result of legal maneuvering. Businesses, too, are encouraging nonsmoking zones. One major hotel chain has recently designated a nonsmoking floor in each of its hotels, to which nonsmoking cleaning or maintenance personnel are assigned. Restaurants in some states have voluntarily designated nonsmoking dining areas, and in other states such areas are required.

A recent exhaustive survey by the U.S. Public Health Service has illuminated the legislative efforts to place limitations on smoking and tobacco products in the United States. This report tallies the 215 bills that were introduced in various state legislatures in 1976, and it describes the 23 bills that were enacted into law. The box score is presented in Table 9.

Table 9
1976 Report Card for State Legislatures*

	Smoking Bills Introduced		Smoking Bills Enacted into Law	
	number of states	number of bills	number of states	number of laws
Limitations on smoking	29	68	4	4
Commerce	33	125	13	16
Smoking & schools	6	7	1	1
Advertising	3	3	0	0
Sales to minors	3	4	0	0
Other	3	8	2	2
TOTAL	41†	215	19†	23

*Adapted from: U.S. Public Health Service. *State Legislation on Smoking and Health*, Atlanta: Center for Disease Control, 1977.
†**Note:** These figures are not totals of bills but, rather, totals of states; certain states introduced or enacted more than one bill each.

It is interesting and instructive to analyze the major categories that various laws fall into and to note the low percentage of bills that became law. Obviously an even longer perspective would be required for a clear picture of legislative efforts to control smoking behavior, but this 1976 report demonstrates the growing awareness on the part of legislators that the public's view of smoking is changing.

In January 1978, Joseph A. Califano, Jr., the secretary of the Department of Health, Education, and Welfare, gave a presentation before the National Interagency Council on Smoking and Health. He announced major new governmental efforts to address issues of smoking and health. This new attack will encompass such things as warning labels, differential cigarette taxing, and primary prevention in youth and will be directed by the newly established Office on Smoking and Health.

Private groups are organizing into an antismoking lobby. For example, Action for Smoking and Health (ASH), an organization designating itself as "the legal action arm of the anti-smoking community," has initiated and advocated legislation protecting the rights of nonsmokers. The overall effect of such public lobbying and legislation may be to reduce the number of situations (signals) for smoking and, conversely, to increase the number of nonsmoking situations. This development should help ex-smokers avoid temptation and maintain abstinence.

References

Business Week, A long strong pitch for cigarettes. April 14, 1975, p. 23.

Fritschler, A. L. *Smoking and politics: Policymaking and the federal bureaucracy* (2nd. ed.). Englewood Cliffs, N.J.: Prentice-Hall, 1975.

Herron, H. R. Socioeconomic effects of increasing state cigarette taxes. In Borgatta, E. F. & Evans, R. R. (eds.), *Smoking, health, and behavior.* Chicago: Aldine, 1968, pp. 263–266.

O'CONNER, J. J. Ad spending for cigarettes dropped 3.9% last year. *Advertising Age*, Nov. 22, 1976, pp. 35 ff.

RAMSTROM, L. M. New ideas in Sweden's tobacco labeling act. *World Smoking & Health*, 1976, *1*, 28–31.

ROSS, W. S. Poison gases in your cigarettes. Part II: Hydrogen cyanide and nitrogen oxides. *Reader's Digest*, 1976, *109*, No. 656 (Dec.), 92–98.

RUSSELL, M. A. H. Changes in cigarette price and consumption by men in Britain, 1946–1971: A preliminary analysis. *British Journal of Preventive and Social Medicine*, 1973, *27*, 1–7.

RUSSELL, M. A. H. Realistic goals for smoking and health: A case for safer smoking. *The Lancet*, 1974, *1*, 254–258.

STENCEL, S. Smoking foes set up drive. *Palo Alto Times,* Jan. 29, 1977, 11.

U. S. DEPARTMENT OF AGRICULTURE. *Annual report on tobacco statistics, 1976.* Washington, D. C.: Agricultural Marketing Service (Statistical Bulletin No. 570), April, 1977.

U. S. PUBLIC HEALTH SERVICE. *State legislation on smoking and health, 1976* (DHEW Publication CDC 77-8331) Atlanta: Center for Disease Control/Bureau of Health Education, 1977.

WHITESIDE, T. Reporter at large: Smoking still. *The New Yorker*, 1974 (Nov. 18), 121–151.

WORLD HEALTH ORGANIZATION. *Smoking and its effects upon health.* Geneva, Switzerland: World Health Organization, 1975. (Technical Report Series 568).

appendix C

Behavioral Treatment of Smoking

REVIEW OF THE LITERATURE

The evidence that cigarette smoking is causally linked to a number of serious physical disorders has given rise to a significant literature describing and evaluating numerous methods of modifying smoking behavior.* Behavior modifiers, who derive their principles and techniques from experimental psychology, have found the study of cigarette

*This section is adapted from a recently published critical review of the literature: Lichtenstein, E., & B. G. Danaher, Modification of smoking behavior: A critical analysis of theory, research, and practice. In Hersen, M., Eisler, R. M., and Miller, P. M. (eds.), *Progress in behavior modification* (vol. 3). New York: Academic Press, 1976, pp. 70–132. Interested readers are referred to this source for more detailed theoretical and methodological analysis of smoking-control research.

smoking of considerable interest. A variety of learning mechanisms can be applied in plausible fashion to smoking. Bernstein (1969, 1970) offers a general behavioral formulation: "In this view, cigarette smoking is maintained by the observable environmental stimuli (including those originating within the body wall) which elicit it and by those which it produces, that is, by a combination of respondent and operant conditioning." He argues for the flexibility of this formulation in that any environmental variable can be considered as long as it is observable and potentially manipulable.

Problems occur in implementing behavioral treatment because cigarette smoking occurs under such a myriad of different stimulus conditions and in association with so many secondary reinforcers that it is very difficult to specify and control functionally relevant operants and respondents. Thus, it is possible, in principle, to apply many different behavioral strategies and tactics, and the researcher-clinician must somehow select the right ones.

A second issue concerns the implications of numerous experimental demonstrations of the reinforcing effects of nicotine on animals and man. One approach is represented by a set of studies demonstrating that humans alter their rate of smoking and rate of puffing in accordance with the nicotine content of their cigarettes (Armitage, 1973, and Jarvik, 1973). A second approach reported by Hutchinson and Emley (1973) is particularly persuasive from a behavioral perspective. Using operant paradigms with both monkeys and men, they show convincingly that nicotine decreases the effects of stressful and unpleasant stimulation. For example, nicotine inhibits pain-elicited aggression, while simultaneously enhancing reactions that permit the organism to reduce or terminate unpleasant or stressful stimuli. In still a third approach, Schachter and his colleagues have conducted a clever and provocative series of studies of the interaction of psychological and pharmacological determinants of smoking

(Schachter, Silverstein, Kozlowski, Perlick, Herman, & Liebling, 1977). Their data support the hypothesis that heavy smokers smoke for nicotine and suggest that the urinary pH mechanism is the biochemical mediator of the stress-smoking relationship. Russell (1976) has summarized the evidence in support of nicotine as a reinforcer and has commented that, "stated plainly, tobacco smoking is a form of drug dependence different but no less strong than that of other addictive drugs" (Russell, 1976, p. 1).

The wide variety of behavioral smoking control strategies precludes neat categorization of the research literature. We have chosen to use two broad, but not mutually exclusive, categories: (1) aversion strategies, which aim at suppressing smoking behavior and usually, but not necessarily, emphasize laboratory sessions and minimize homework assignments; (2) self-control strategies which emphasize homework assignments and usually, but not necessarily, minimize aversive control.

Treatment effectiveness needs to be evaluated from both a relative and absolute perspective. By a *relative perspective* we mean comparisons between specific behavioral treatments and attention-placebo, nonbehavioral, or no-treatment comparison groups. By an *absolute perspective*, we mean the amount of smoking cessation or reduction achieved. A treatment strategy may show statistical superiority, especially to a non-treated control, while producing relatively little abstinence or only modest reduction in smoking rates.

The absolute perspective requires a frame of reference in order to interpret such phrases as "relatively little abstinence" or "unimpressive reduction in smoking rates." Hunt and Bespalec (1974) summarized data from 89 smoking-control studies representing all manner of approaches. Figure 16 is adapted from their report and displays both the percentage of abstainers and percentage of baseline for the

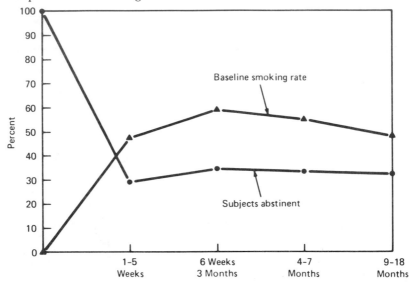

Figure 16
Relapse Rate in Smoking Treatment

Reprinted with permission from E. Lichtenstein & B. G. Danaher's Modification of smoking behavior: A critical analysis of theory, research, and practice. In M. Herson, R. M. Eisler, & P. M. Miller (eds.), *Progress in Behavior Modification* (vol. 3). New York: Academic Press, 1976.

subjects at varying follow-up intervals. It can be seen that most relapses occur during the first month after treatment and that the relapse curve is a negatively accelerated one that breaks sharply at the three- to six-month point. The percentage of abstinent subjects asymptotes in the 20 to 30 percent range, and smoking rates asymptote around 60 percent of baseline. Hunt and Bespalec's cautions about wide variability in sample size, treatment procedures, and reporting techniques should be kept in mind. Also, the curves are based only on subjects who achieve abstinence at termination, thus yielding an overly optimistic picture of total program effectiveness. McFall and Hammen (1971) reviewed a much smaller subset of behavioral studies. At the four- or six-month follow-up, percentage of baseline smoking averaged about 75 percent of baseline, and the percentage of abstinent subjects ranged from 9 to 17 percent, with a mean of 13 percent.

AVERSION STRATEGIES

As with other intrinsically rewarding problem behaviors such as alcoholism, aversive strategies are frequently applied to smoking control. Three major kinds of aversive stimuli have been used: electric shock, cigarette smoke itself, and covert sensitization (imaginal stimulation).

Electric-shock Aversion

In a previous review of the smoking literature (Lichtenstein & Keutzer, 1971), it was concluded that laboratory-administered shock was ineffective because "human [subjects] appear to be all too capable of discriminating between shock and no-shock situations, and the hoped-for generalization never materialized" (p. 63). With one exception, studies using shock since that review suggest little need to revise that statement.

A comprehensive study by Russell, Armstrong, and Patel (1976) is representative. Russell (1970) previously reported some encouraging results with electric shock and well-motivated smokers. (Six of nine subjects, out of 23 original referrals, who completed a conditioning program were abstinent at one year follow-up.) In a well-controlled extension of this work, 70 heavy smokers (mean = 32 cigarettes per day) were randomly assigned to one of five conditions: (1) electric shock contingent on smoking; (2) noncontingent electric shock; (3) no-shock smoking sessions to control for possible satiation or negative practice effects; (4) simple support and attention from therapists; and (5) no treatment. Treated subjects were seen for 10 sessions with 20 shock trials per session. All four treatments were significantly more effective than the no-treatment condition. Contingent and non-contingent shock groups did not differ and were no more successful than the no-shock or simple attention groups. A conditioned motor response was demonstrable in 19 of 28 shock subjects, but it was irrelevant to treatment outcome.

Most studies of laboratory shock yield weak results in either an absolute sense, a relative sense, or both (Andrews, 1970, Conway, 1977, and Levine, 1974). The striking exception is a recent study by Dericco, Brigham, and Garlington (1977). In a well-controlled study, shock was clearly more effective than either satiation or a variation of covert sensitization. Sixteen of 20 subjects in the shock conditions stopped smoking and remained abstinent through a one-year follow-up. The number of sessions and shock intensity were much greater than in other shock studies, and this may both account for the observed treatment effect and also limit practical application.

While contingent shock for smoking behavior in the laboratory (unless unusually intense and prolonged) does not by itself usually reduce smoking behavior, it is still possible that shock augmented by other procedures may prove useful. Chapman, Smith, and Layden (1971) combined daily shock sessions with intensive "self-management" training. Six of 11 subjects in one of their studies were abstinent at the twelve-month follow-up. The effects of the self-management training were not evaluated and may have been responsible for treatment effects.

Transfer to the natural environment remains a problem for many office-bound treatment methods, especially aversion. Some of the work on alcoholism (Vogler, Lunde,

Johnson, & Martin, 1970) attempts to overcome this difficulty by surrounding the subject with many cues and stimuli related to his drinking (for example, a simulated barroom situation). This has not been accomplished with smoking, probably because smoking—in contrast to drinking—can occur in such a wide variety of contexts that it is practically impossible to simulate all or most of them. If one could condition the thoughts, images, or covert verbalizations that smokers are assumed to emit prior to or during the smoking chain, then we might hope for better generalization of conditioning effects. Steffy, Meichenbaum & Best (1970) formed four groups: (1) overt verbalization with smoking; (2) covert verbalization with smoking; (3) overt verbalization with nonsmoking; and (4) insight control. Contrary to their expectation, the covert verbalization with smoking group was significantly more successful in smoking reduction than the other groups. However, the absolute level of reduction was not impressive, and the use of relatively light smokers and a fairly high attrition rate further qualify interpretation of this study.

Berecz (1972) had subjects self-administer shock in the laboratory while they were either actually smoking or just imagining themselves smoking. The imagined smoking condition was significantly better for heavy smokers, who smoked 20 or more cigarettes a day, and comparable to the actual smoking condition for what Berecz termed moderate smokers, who averaged about 13 cigarettes per day. Berecz (1974) has argued forcefully for the superiority of using shock on cognitions about the target behavior rather than the behavior itself. We agree that cognitions deserve greater attention, and some of the self-control strategies reviewed below attempt to do so. Berecz (1974) presents several pilot cases in support of his contention, but more controlled research is clearly needed.

Another approach to the problem of transfer is to

employ apparatus to administer shock contingently in the smoker's natural environment: a special cigarette pack that automatically causes a painful shock when opened. Powell and Azrin (1968) varied the intensity of the shock with three subjects and found, consistent with laboratory data, that smoking reduction was directly related to the intensity of the punishing stimulus. It was also found that the greater the intensity of the shock, the less time subjects used the apparatus. In addition, some subjects withdrew from the study. However, prior to their selection for the study, these subjects had not indicated any desire to stop smoking. It is possible that with motivated subjects the negative side effects observed would be greatly diminished.

Cigarette-smoke Aversion

The choice of cigarette smoke as the aversive stimulus in smoking treatment may be a particularly appropriate one (Danaher & Lichtenstein, 1974). Excessive smoke affects many of the endogenous cues that characterize smoking, thereby increasing the impact of aversive therapy. Wilson and Davison (1969) summarized the animal literature indicating potent effects for aversion where target responses and associated aversive stimuli exhibit significant topographical similarities; they contend that this phenomenon has important implications for the choice of aversive stimuli in clinical research. Cigarette smoke as an aversive stimulus has been used in two major ways: rapid smoking and satiation.

Rapid Smoking

Requiring subjects to smoke rapidly and continually or blowing warm, stale smoke in subjects' faces is an increasingly popular aversion procedure. Early work on rapid smoking-blown smoky air was unimpressive except for some work by Lublin and Joslyn (1968). Using several of Lublin's procedures, a group at the University of Oregon initiated an influential set of studies.

In the first study (Schmahl et al., 1972), 28 habituated smokers received either warm, smoky air, or warm, mentholated air (a presumed control group) in a paradigm which required them to smoke until they could tolerate no further cigarettes. Both groups puffed at a rapid rate, once every six seconds, received considerable social reinforcement, and were given high expectations of success. Rather than participating in a fixed number of sessions, subjects were seen until they were abstinent and felt they could control their smoking. All subjects were abstinent at termination, after an average of eight sessions. Sixteen of the 25 subjects were abstinent at the six-month follow-up, but there were no differences between the smoky-air and menthol-air groups.

In a second study (Lichtenstein et al., 1973), the social and relationship variables were kept constant, though at a relatively enriched level, and the nature and degree of the aversive stimulation were varied. Subjects were randomly assigned to one of four treatment groups: warm, smoky air plus rapid smoking (the same treatment given experimental subjects in the first study); warm, smoky air only; rapid smoking only; or attention-placebo. Three experimenters, also randomly assigned, saw each subject individually for an average of 7.2 sessions, and follow-up data were obtained for six months post treatment. There were no differences among experimenters. All subjects but one were abstinent at termination, and 21 subjects remained abstinent six months later. A significant treatment group by follow-up interval interaction was observed, and found to be attributable to the attention-placebo group's steeper relapse curve. The three aversion groups were very similar in performance; six of 10 subjects in each were abstinent at six-month follow-up. This study indicated that the aversive stimulation per se contributed to the treatment effect, but there was no additive effect from subjects' smoking rapidly while smoke was blown into their faces. Rapid smoking was clearly just as effective as the smoke-blowing apparatus. While some studies have continued to combine rapid smoking and smoky air (Best, 1975; Flaxman, in press; Lublin & Barry, 1973; and Lublin & Joslyn, 1968), in the majority of subsequent research, the smoke-blowing apparatus has been dropped in favor of the more convenient rapid-smoking procedure.

One of the factors that seemed particularly important in this early research was the role of interpersonal contact and persuasion. In a third study (Harris & Lichtenstein, 1971), the level of aversive stimulation was kept constant—using the rapid-smoking procedure, while three social or relationship factors believed important were varied in the treatment situation. Subjects receiving the same high levels of social interaction and relationship were about as successful as smokers in our previous work, imdependent of being seen individually or in small groups. Subjects given the same aversive procedure but in a barren social context, were significantly less successful, both at termination and follow-up. Eight of 18 subjects in this deprived group were not smoking at termination, and their posttreatment relapse rate was significantly steeper than for the enriched groups.

It was reasoned that many of these subjects might still be experiencing strong urges to smoke and that continuation of treatment to the point of eliminating urges might improve long-term abstinence rates. Weinrobe and Lichtenstein (1975) directly investigated this point by instructing smokers to self-monitor urges as well as smoking throughout the course of treatment. Twenty-nine smokers received rapid-smoking aversion treatment until they achieved abstinence and were terminated when they reported no smoking urges or when they still reported urges but believed they could control them. As hypothesized, smoking rates for subjects reporting urges (N = 11) were significantly higher. Interestingly, the no-smoking plus zero-urge subjects required fewer sessions than did the subjects using only the smoking criterion. The overall results of this study were quite consistent with the previous three. All subjects were abstinent at termination; at three months after treatment, 17 of 29 subjects were abstinent and the percentage of baseline smoking was 28 per cent.

Figure 17 presents follow-up data on subjects from the four studies who experienced rapid smoking and contingent warmth. All subjects from the first study (Schmahl et al.,

Figure 17
Follow-up Data on Smoking Rate
for Aversive Smokers

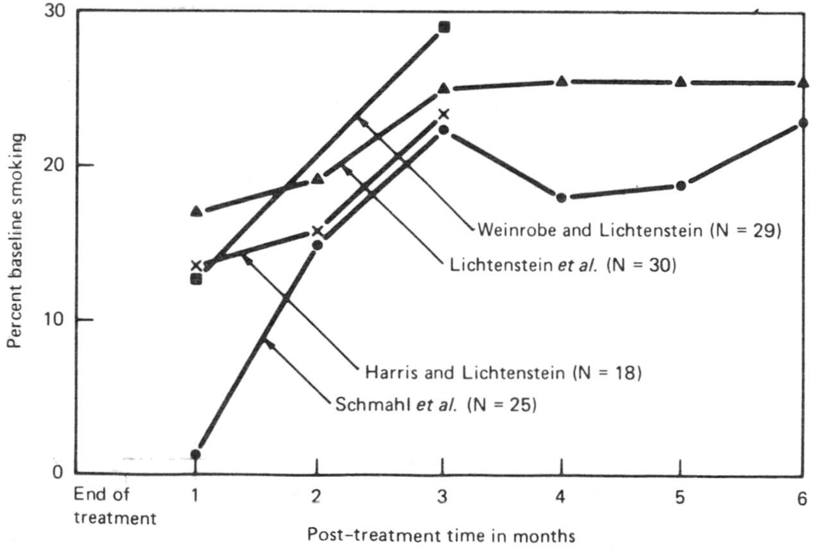

Weinrobe and Lichtenstein (N = 29)

Lichtenstein *et al.* (N = 30)

Harris and Lichtenstein (N = 18)

Schmahl *et al.* (N = 25)

Reprinted with permission from E. Lichtenstein & B. G. Danaher, Modification of smoking behavior: A critical analysis of theory, research, and practice. In M. Hersen, R. M. Eisler, & P. M. Miller (eds.), *Progress in Behavior Modification* (vol. 3). New York: Academic Press, 1976.

1972), the three aversion groups from Lichtenstein et al. (1973), the high-social-condition subjects from the Harris and Lichtenstein (1971) study, and all of the subjects from Weinrobe and Lichtenstein (1975) study are included. Given the differences in subjects, the different experimenters, and the variations in procedure, these data seem remarkably consistent. The relapse curves tend to flatten out around the third month, and relapse is clearly most pronounced during the first three months and usually during the first month. The shapes of the relapse curves are quite similar to Hunt and Bespalec's (1974) summary curve depicted in Figure 16. However, the heights of the four rapid-smoking relapse curves are considerably lower.

Rapid smoking has received perhaps the most intensive investigation of any contemporary smoking-control procedure. Almost 30 studies have been reported, including many controlled investigations. Danaher (1977,a) has reviewed this literature and has drawn attention to these factors: (1) importance of cognitively rehearsing the unpleasant experiences as a central aspect of treatment; (2) the importance of the interpersonal treatment context and the possible detrimental effects of group treatment, that is, closely affiliated groups relying too heavily upon mutual support and encouragement so that one member's resumption of the smoking habit may actually set the occasion for a more general recidivism; and (3) the instances where rapid smoking has been combined with self-control procedures (to be described later in this review). Overall, rapid smoking appears to be the most effective treatment option available. Most comparative investigations have shown that it is at least as powerful as alternative treatment procedures, and sometimes it has been strikingly more effective. As might be expected in replication of earlier work, important changes in procedure that may have lessened the overall treatment impact have been made. Danaher (1977,a) has outlined these changes and clinical efforts.

An important consideration in the use of rapid smoking is the need for *medical screening* and for informing subjects of potential physical risks involved. Cigarette smoking, largely by increasing the body's level of nicotine and carbon monoxide in the blood (COHb), accelerates and stresses the cardiovascular system; rapid smoking intensifies these stressful effects. Lichtenstein and Glasgow (1977) have summarized the available data on the risk of rapid smoking and concluded that the quantitative impact of rapid smoking has not proved to be as great as feared. They estimate that approximately 35,000 participants have been exposed to the procedure without serious ill effects. Nevertheless, the need for screening out symptomatic persons is an important restriction in the use of rapid smoking.

Satiation

Overdoing any behavior probably reduces its attractiveness. This fundamental principle has led to the development of a procedure known as satiation. In satiation, the smoker is instructed to greatly increase the usual daily consumption of cigarettes—sometimes doubling or even tripling consumption. No specific instructions are given as to how or when this smoking is to occur, only that the amount of smoking should be increased. Satiation is especially convenient in that it requires no apparatus and is carried out by the subject in his natural environment. However, it requires medical-screening safeguards because doubling or tripling one's smoking for several days would stress the cardiovascular system much like rapid smoking.

Two reports by Resnick (1968a, 1968b) indicate very encouraging results. In the more extensive study (Resnick, 1968b), both satiation groups showed significantly more reduction in smoking than did controls; at the four-month follow-up, 25 of the 40 subjects in the two satiation groups were abstinent, compared with only four of 20 in the control group. Resnick supplied no data concerning how faithfully subjects carried out the satiation procedure. His subjects were young, relatively light smokers, and it has been suggested that his control group did not receive a plausible attention-placebo procedure (Marston & McFall, 1971). Nevertheless, the impressive absolute results and the efficiency of the procedure stimulated a number of efforts to replicate and extend the satiation procedure.

Unfortunately, the overwhelming weight of evidence on satiation since Resnick's original studies is clearly negative. In two studies that compared several treatments, one of which included an attention-placebo group, satiation yielded neither significant between-group differences nor impressive reduction or cessation data (Marston & McFall, 1971, and McCallum, 1971). In two studies that were intended essentially as replications of Resnick's study with methodological improvement, the results were again clearly negative: The satiation groups were not significantly superior to control groups, and the absolute rates of smoking cessation or reduction were not noteworthy (Claiborn, Lewis, & Humble, 1972, and Sushinsky, 1972). Lando (1976) instructed subjects to engage in excessive smoking both in the laboratory and between sessions in their natural environment. Satiation subjects were no more successful than a slow-smoking control group that engaged in neither excessive nor rapid smoking. There have been five relatively unequivocal failures to replicate Resnick's successful employment of satiation. Therefore, the effectiveness of the procedure by itself seems very much in doubt. Several more recent studies (Lando, 1977; Best, Owen, & Trentadue, in press; and Delahunt & Curran, 1976) using satiation have reported more impressive results, but in every case the aversive-smoke procedure was combined with self-control procedures. The potential for combination treatment packages will be discussed later.

The data indicate that satiation is a less effective treatment procedure than rapid smoking, although the two techniques seem functionally similar. Rapid smoking typically has been laboratory-administered during several treatment sessions involving a persuasive interpersonal relationship. In contrast, satiation studies have repeated Resnick's procedure of employing very minimal treatment time and experimenter contact or have intentionally minimized interpersonal persuasiveness. It is possible that the apparent superiority of rapid smoking is, in part, a function of variables such as treatment time and interpersonal persuasiveness.

Another possible factor involved is the relative emphasis on cognitive focusing and revivification in the two procedures. Rapid smoking typically calls for subjects to focus on negative experiences during the trials and immediately thereafter. Satiation in the natural environment appears to avoid involving such explicit instructional sets to use cognitions and thus may not facilitate generalization or maintenance.

Aversion by Covert Sensitization (imaginal stimulation)

Covert sensitization reflects aversion therapy's growing concern with cognitive antecedents and consequences (Cautela, 1970). In this procedure, both the target behavior and the aversive stimulus are presented imaginally by asking the smoker to first visualize getting ready to smoke and then to imagine the experience of nausea and vomiting. An escape-relief dimension is introduced at this point by instructing the smoker to imagine feeling better while turning away and rejecting the available cigarettes. The subject is usually given training and practice in the procedure in the laboratory and may be encouraged or instructed to carry it out in his natural environment, thus permitting it to be used as a self-control procedure. The portability of the procedure and its relative safety—physical risk and discomfort are minimal—are a considerable practical advantage.

Wagner and Bragg (1970) found that a combination of systematic desensitization and covert sensitization was superior to either procedure alone. This was a well-controlled study, but the absolute degree of smoking reduction and cessation was not large. Sachs, Bean, and Morrow (1970) found covert sensitization to be superior to self-control and attention-placebo groups, although again the differences were not substantial. Sachs et al. attempted to reduce demand characteristics by instructing subjects not to use their own effort to facilitate treatment, but this directive may have confused their subjects. In several other studies varying in adequacy of controls (Fuhrer, 1971; Lawson & May, 1970; McCallum, 1971; Sipich, Russell, & Tobias, 1974; Weiss, 1974; and Wisocki & Rooney, 1974), either covert sensitization was less effective than other treatments or controls or the absolute smoking reduction achieved was relatively minimal.

The overall evidence in support of covert sensitization in the modification of smoking behavior appears to be relatively weak. The economy and portability of the procedure suggest, however, that it deserves additional empirical study.

Limitations of Aversion

Aversion therapy has a number of inherent limitations. Many investigators are concerned on esthetic and ethical grounds. The physical riskiness of certain aversive procedures such as rapid smoking, limits their general application and may prevent their use with individuals most in need of treatment.

A more general question concerning aversive strategies relates to what we can fairly expect of them. Bandura (1969) specifies that the optimal application of counterconditioning involves the reduction of the targeted response, with the concurrent acceleration of suitable substitute behaviors (incompatible at best). However, acceptable substitutes to smoking are not easily found, and, as the later discussion of self-control packages suggests, those substitutes that have been identified have not evidenced particularly strong effects.

A modification of the perspective on aversion therapy seems in order. Certain kinds of aversion do appear to be quite successful in producing short-term cessation. An increasingly evident conclusion, however, is that cognitive variables must be considered in more detail if initial cessation is to be succesfully prolonged to the point of long-term abstinence. The rehearsal of unpleasant imagery—of remembering the unpleasant experiences that occur in aversion therapy—may be a key component. (Recall the earlier discussion of rapid smoking.) Bandura (1969) has argued that it is this imaginal revivification of the aversion that enables the individual to resist subsequent temptations and successfully manage his or her behavior. Viewing current aversion strategies as having the limited goal of producing short-term cessation should sharpen the search for other principles and methods that will enable greater maintenance of change.

SELF-CONTROL STRATEGIES

The second major class of smoking treatments can be categorized loosely as those involving *self-control*. Self-control includes those procedures which the client applies in situ to change some aspect of his own behavior. Self-control includes completely self-administered treatment programs as well as those more common programs in which the client works closely with a consultant-therapist during the training phase. The focus of self-control on the individual-as-change-agent and on the application of the intervention tactics at home, often by means of homework assignments, practically ensures that treatment will have some significant impact on the client's real world.

With one major modification, we have followed the general outline of self-control provided by Thoresen and Mahoney (1974) in employing *environmental planning* and *behavioral programming* as two major categories. We employ a third category, *cognitive control*, to encompass a set of procedures which seem to combine elements of both planning and programming. The major self-control strategies and associated tactics are shown in Table 10.

Table 10
Self-control Strategies and Tactics

I. Environmental Planning	II. Behavioral Programming	III. Cognitive Controls

A. stimulus control
  1. increased stimulus
    interval
  2. hierarchical
    reduction
  3. deprived-response
    performance
	A. self-reward	A. self-instruction
		  (coverant control)

B. contingency
  contracting
  1. deposit systems
  2. social contracts
	B. self-
	  punishment
		B. imagery
		  rehearsal

Environmental Planning

One major class of self-control procedures, based upon research evidence from the animal laboratory, seeks to reduce smoking by rearranging the prevailing circumstances under which smoking occurs. The client formulates a game plan, by which he arranges his environment in ways that will contribute to his effort to stop smoking. These arrangements are made in advance, and they may relieve the client of immediate responsibility for responding to his smoking urges. Instead, he need only remain vigilant and adhere to his carefully constructed plan, while preprogrammed environmental forces operate to reduce the frequency of his smoking, at least in theory. Two major types of environmental planning with the aim of reducing smoking will be reviewed: stimulus control and contingency management.

Stimulus Control

Stimulus control has been the basis for a set of clinical procedures that seek to control maladaptive behavior by systematically changing the usual stimulus situations in which the targeted response occurs. From this perspective, smoking is viewed as having become linked to a variety of specific environmental and internal events that have come to serve as discriminative stimuli, or cues, for the smoking response. The act of smoking in association with these internal-external cues has been reinforced on some partial schedule, so that the presence of the cues, for instance, a glass of beer, cup of coffee, or feeling of tension, becomes associated with strong, subjectively experienced urges to smoke. The prevailing stimulus-response conditions are generally altered by means of a two-step stimulus-control program: (a) Smoking is initially restricted to novel situations in order to extinguish the power of prior cues, and (b) the novel stimuli are subsequently faded, thereby encouraging a corresponding reduction or elimination of smoking. Important features of the stimulus-control approach are the emphasis on gradual reduction rather than immediate cessation and the client's responsibility for carrying out the treatment plan in his natural environment. Three major strategies for achieving stimulus control of smoking have been devised:

Increasing the Stimulus Interval. This strategy allows for continued smoking but limits its performance to particular times which are signaled by some cueing device. Once well established, the new smoking cue is gradually thinned or faded by simply increasing the time interval between its presentations.

In an elegant example of this approach, Azrin and Powell (1968) utilized a cigarette case that automatically locked itself for a period of time following the removal of a cigarette. Distinctive stimuli, both tactile and auditory, signaled when the device could be opened again and came to serve as the cue for smoking, particularly as the interval between locking and unlocking was increased. The smoking rates of five heavy smokers were gradually reduced from about two and a half packs a day to half a pack a day by systematically lengthening the intervals. The procedure was relatively inoffensive to the participants, but their smoking rates returned to normal after the apparatus was withdrawn. These subjects were recruited and had not sought help for their smoking.

Other smoking-on-cue programs have used simple pocket timers and have sometimes varied the interval schedule. These studies have revealed weak absolute results and substantial dropout rates. Subjects consistently have found it difficult to reduce gradually to less than 12 cigarettes a day (Upper & Meredith, 1971; Bernard & Efran, 1972; Claiborn et al., 1972; Levinson, Shapiro, Schwartz & Tursky, 1971; and Shapiro, Tursky, Schwartz, & Schnidman, 1971).

Hierarchical Reduction. In a second major approach to stimulus control, subjects are asked to monitor their smoking activity and identify situations in which smoking would enjoy a high and low probability. A hierarchy, based on either the presumed difficulty of reducing smoking in a situation or the enjoyment from smoking in the situation, is developed. The subject then reduces or eliminates his smoking in cumulative and progressive fashion from the easiest to the hardest situations in the hierarchy. This method has also yielded weak results (Gutmann & Marston, 1967; Sachs et al., 1970; and Marston & McFall, 1971).

Flaxman (in press) hypothesized that gradual reduction may be appropriate to a point at which abrupt cessation is necessary. This reasoning is consistent with the findings that twelve cigarettes a day is a difficult barrier for subjects on a gradual-reduction program. In a carefully designed study, all subjects received self-control instructions and were assigned to the following experimental conditions: gradual quitting with a hierarchy method; partial-gradual quitting in which the hierarchy program was used to cut back gradually until half the steps were completed or smoking had been reduced to half of baseline, at which level immediate cessation was required; target-date quitting, in which subjects were instructed to choose a date approximately two weeks after start of treatment, by which time cessation was required; and immediate quitting, with abstinence required following the first treatment session. Half of the subjects also received aversive conditioning. Six-month follow-up results clearly favored target-date cessation over hierarchical reduction and immediate quitting. Process analyses indicated that few subjects in the partial-gradual reduction condition progressed to abrupt cessation.

Deprived-response Performance. The third major application of stimulus control progressively narrows the discriminative stimuli for smoking by delimiting the circumstances in which smoking is allowed. This procedure requires that all smoking occur in a deprived setting or one devoid of all possible distractions and accompanying reinforcers. A common example is smoking only while seated in a "smoking chair" located in a subject's garage. The deprived-response program also includes significant aspects of self-punishment. Removing oneself from an ongoing social interaction in order to withdraw to a smoking chair can be viewed as self-imposed time-out procedure. Two N=1 case reports have presented successful application of the procedure to smoking (Nolan, 1968, and Roberts, 1969). In these cases, however, the subject was either the experimenter's wife or the experimenter himself. In both cases smoking cessation occurred abruptly toward the end and appeared to be a function of processes other than stimulus-control. Furthermore, these successes were not replicated in a better controlled project by Karen and Bogardus (1973), who found both high attrition and consistent return to baseline among those subjects who participated. Although results of direct tests of the smoking-chair technique have been mixed, the procedure has been employed in numerous self-control packages, probably because of its convenience and face validity.

In contrast to reported successes in controling other behavioral excesses, stimulus-control approaches to smoking reduction and cessation have not been at all impressive. Subjects appear to find many of the procedures burdensome and terminate treatment. Gradual reduction below a certain level, approximately 12 cigarettes per day, appears to be quite difficult, and this may be a level at which the primary reinforcement of nicotine becomes paramount. Gradual quitting may serve to establish an aperiodic reinforcement schedule which interferes with extinction (Flaxman, in press), or it may serve to increase the reinforcement value and thereby the attractiveness of the remaining cigarettes. Stimulus-control procedures have continued to be popular, however, perhaps as a result of the persuasiveness of the proposed underlying model or the relatively painless method, which allows smoking but limits only the situations in which it can occur.

Contingency Contracting

Contingency contracting refers to arrangements (contracts) made by a smoker with another individual to help modify his smoking behavior. Within the usual practice of contingency contracting, the smoker makes arrangements so that he need not be concerned with the appropriate administration of contingent rewards or punishments. The function of providing consequation is the major responsibility of the individual or agency specified in the contract. The smoker is completely familiar with the terms of the smoking contract, however, and is aware of the costs attached to transgression. Contracting as a method of smoking control has taken two major forms: deposit systems and social contracts.

Deposit Systems. Deposits are commonly used to promote participation and gain compliance with program tasks and assignments. Less frequently, deposit return is tied contingently to smoking cessation or reduction. Deposits are usually monetary although material possessions that lend themselves to partial repayment, for example, a record collection, may be employed. Tokens may also be used to facilitate the assignment of tangible rewards for appropriate reduction or abstinence (Bornstein, Carmody, Relinger, Zohn, Devine, &

Bugge, 1975). Deposit-contract systems include a strong element of punishment (response cost), because portions of the deposit may be forfeited by transgression. Although both reinforcement and punishment complement each other, it seems clear that the sustained threat of losing one's deposit provides the dominant influence (Tighe & Elliott, 1968).

Two studies present clear examples of the deposit system with the major controlling tactic of returning portions of subjects' deposits contingent on progressively longer periods of abstinence. Elliott and Tighe (1968) found that 84 percent of their subjects were abstinent following treatment and 37.5 percent remained abstinent through relatively long follow-up periods. In a more complete factorial design, Winett (1973) found that contingent repayment produced significantly greater smoking cessation than did noncontingent repayment schedules. At six-month follow-up, 50 percent versus 23.5 percent of the subjects were abstinent in the contingent and noncontingent group respectively. Lando (1976) combined aversion, that is, satiation, with a contract-deposit method and found good initial results but considerable relapse. Contingency contracts have also been imposed in a self-control program (Spring, Sipich, Trimble, & Goeckner, (in press). After treatment, contingency-contract subjects abstained more than noncontingent or no-contract subjects, but group differences washed out at follow-up. In sum, contingency contracting appears to offer a simple and economical method of producing cessation and may be grafted onto other treatment strategies.

Social Contracts. Although efforts to stop smoking often include elements of public announcement mixed with encouragement and support from family members, friends, and associates, one line of smoking research has attempted to make more explicit use of these social contingencies as a means for motivating reduction or abstinence. The emphasis on social contracts ranges from studies in which subjects have simply made public announcements that they are trying to quit, which presumably set in motion appropriate social consequation (Tighe & Elliott, 1968), to cases in which friends and family members are described as having acted as reinforcers for successful smoking reduction (Bornstein et al., 1975; and Lawson & May, 1970).

Married couples who want to stop smoking together present potentially powerful opportunities for investigating social contracting as a smoking-control tactic. Two studies, neither with formal control groups, dealt with married couples as a means of rewarding nonsmoking. Nehemkis and Lichtenstein (1971) trained a small number of married couples so that spouses reciprocally reinforced each other for successfully meeting graduated reduction goals. Cumulative reduction—as well as cessation for about half the couples—was achieved during treatment and short-term follow-up, but a six-month follow-up indicated considerable relapse. Gutmann and Marston (1967) were notably less successful in their effort with graduated reduction in married couples, perhaps because they chose to use smoking as a reward for reduction.

Another lightly investigated aspect of social contracting as a means of smoking control is the "buddy system." By systematically programming contracts between smokers and training them in appropriate verbal praise and contingent rewards, it may be possible to increase treatment effectiveness (Janis & Hoffmann, 1970).

Environmental-planning efforts to control smoking have had mixed results. Stimulus-control procedures fail to produce cessation in most cases. Contingency contracting has shown more promise, but results have not been uniform. One pervasive problem in this research has been the implicit assumption that the gradual reduction of smoking is synonymous with the gradual approximation of nonsmoking. Nonsmoking precludes operational definition, because it describes lack of behavior rather than the operation of some alternative response. Research should be directed toward identifying and systematically applying substitute behaviors that will both replace smoking and make its resumption unlikely.

Behavioral Programming

Thoresen and Mahoney (1974) have stressed that these instances of behavioral programming usually occur after performance of the target behavior. In the present discussion, however, the temporal aspect of the presentation is less critical than the fact that the individual initiates and self-administers the controlling strategy.

Two categories of behavioral programming can be traced directly to the literature of operant learning, in that the emphasis is on self-reward and self-punishment.

Self-reward. In one strategy, the smoker assigns a self-reward contingent upon successfully avoiding smoking. Self-reward lends itself to programs stressing abstinence, those aimed at gradual reduction by means of a changing criterion design, and those emphasizing the acquisition of nonsmoking skills. While these straightforward applications of self-reward could stand as treatment programs in their own right, they have been used generally as motivational systems in multifaceted treatment programs emphasizing a number of various strategies. It should be noted that self-reward regimens need not be limited to tangible rewards, because self-evaluatory statements play an important role in the modification of smoking behavior.

Self-punishment. The converse of assigning rewards for appropriate behavior is the application of punishments for transgressions of a self-imposed standard. Axelrod, Hall, Weis, and Rohrer (1974), for example, instructed a smoker to tear up a dollar bill every time he smoked a cigarette while, in another case, the smoker contributed 25 cents to a charity for each smoke. These response-cost procedures produced mixed results; the dollar procedure produced abstinence in 50 days without resumption, while the 25 cent-contribution subject continued to smoke. While group studies with factorial designs are needed to identify the possible active ingredients suggested by these case reports, it seems safe to conclude that 25-cent fines for smoking are probably not sufficiently aversive. In one suggested alternative, the donation is sent to the organization most hated by the smoker (Watson & Tharp, 1972). Irrespective of the method used, it seems clear that strong aversive consequences are required to counteract smoking.

Stronger aversion has been involved in the self-application of some of the procedures discussed in an earlier section, including rapid smoking (Kopel, 1974) and shock (Ober, 1968). Technically, any of the self-administered or homework versions of what are otherwise office-bound procedures (rapid smoking and covert sensitization) are examples of self-punishment. The fact that their in-situ administration sometimes fails to follow the target behavior does not negate this label. As noted above, self-administered shock or rapid smoking has produced effective posttreatment suppression of smoking. ·

Cognitive Controls

A third category of self-control involves the client's explicit manipulation of his cognitive behavior (thoughts, self-instruction, imagery rehearsal, etc.) as a smoking-control strategy. Changing the manner in which smokers think before and after smoking has provided an arena for vigorous

research. Cognitions incompatible with smoking may be
practiced in a clinic (Chapman et al., 1971 emotional response routine), in the form of scheduled homework assignments (Miller & Gimpl, 1971), or on an ad-libitum basis
to combat smoking urges.

Self-instruction (coverant control)

To date, the greatest research effort in the area of cognitive control of smoking has been directed at a particular set
of procedures known as "coverant control." Homme (1965)
coined the word coverant to refer to covert operant behavior
or thoughts. The general procedure instructs the client to
think about or give himself two compelling reasons (covert
statements) focusing on different aspects of his attempt to
stop smoking. The first statement, an antismoking thought,
presents some aversive aspect of continued smoking, and the
second thought, which is pro-nonsmoking, emphasizes the
benefits that follow sustained nonsmoking. The strategy is
thus initiated when an urge to smoke is experienced and is
followed by the self-assignment of some other rewarding activity.

The purpose of coverant control is to eliminate smoking
by strengthening self-statements and associated cognitions
that are incompatible with its performance. The procedure is
safe, requires no apparatus, and can be tailored to individual
thoughts, beliefs, and feelings of the smoker. These factors
may account for its relative popularity. A number of studies
have compared coverant-control strategies with several other
behavioral treatments or with appropriate self-monitoring or
attention-placebo control methods (Keutzer, 1968; Lawson &
May, 1970; Rutner, 1967; and Tooley & Pratt, 1967). They
have received extensive review elsewhere (Mahoney, 1974).

Less well reviewed studies have also appeared. Johnson

(1968) found coverant control to be superior, both at end of treatment and at the three- and six-month follow-ups, to an attention-placebo control. On the other hand, a breath-holding group—subjects hold their breath until it becomes mildly uncomfortable whenever they have an urge to smoke—performed about as well as the coverant-control groups. Hark (1970) found coverant control to be signficantly better than a no-contact control group but not superior to a nondirective discussion group. Gordon (1971) examined the effects of timing the negative coverant: (a) prior to touch-ing a package of cigarettes, (b) after lighting but before inhal-ing a cigarette, or (c) prior to any high-probability behavior. An attention-placebo control was also included. Only one-month follow-up data were reported, and these indicated no differences among groups. All groups demonstrated sig-nificant smoking reduction, and the magnitude of the reduc-tion was relatively large in comparison with results from many behavioral studies. Danaher and Lichtenstein (1974b) compared the efficacy of various combinations of cues and consequences within the coverant-control framework. Pro-cess data showed subjects carried out the treatment proce-dure more faithfully when they assigned themselves valued rewards. Consistent with other research, however, no sig-nificant differences between coverant control and the attention-placebo method emerged at the eight-month follow-up. Although successful case reports exist (Danaher, 1976), the controlled-research evidence argues that the clini-cal effectiveness of coverant control appears to be minimal.

Subvocal and imaginal procedures may, however, be useful in enhancing the client's commitment to change be-havior and carry out program requirements (Marston & Feldman, 1972). Many smokers have experienced past fail-ures and frustrations in trying to stop, and they emit to themselves such negative covert statements as "I guess I'm just addicted" or "I can't do anything when the urge to smoke hits me." Further clinical and research experimentation appears necessary in order to develop the necessary principles and technology to deal with these covert-control processes.

CONTROLLED SMOKING

With rare exceptions (Azrin & Powell, 1968), abstinence has been the treatment goal in all studies reviewed. This is based on a widely shared assumption that confirmed smokers cannot maintain a low and presumably safe rate of smoking. Clinical experience with smokers who try to cut down and evidence for nicotine dependence seem to support this assumption. Recently the required abstinence for smokers has been questioned in much the same way as the controlled consumption of alcohol (Miller & Muñoz, 1976).

Frederiksen and Peterson (1976; Frederiksen, Peterson & Murphy, 1976) have proposed that safer smoking can be achieved by controlling three major components: substance, rate, and topography. Substance refers to changing the kind of tobacco used in order to lower tar or nicotine; rate refers to reducing the number of cigarettes smoked; and topography involves changing how much smoke is inhaled, how many puffs per cigarette are taken, and how much of the cigarette is smoked. Frederiksen and Peterson have reported success in training subjects to achieve substance, rate, and topography changes. The long-term stability of such changes remains to be determined. It is also necessary to watch for compensatory smoking if one or two components are changed. For example, a reduction in rate may lead to deeper inhalation; switching to a pipe may lead to inhaling the pipe smoke. The issue of safer smoking is discussed in broader perspective in *Appendix a.*

Broad-spectrum Treatment Packages

An emerging trend in smoking control has been to combine procedures within what is known as a treatment package. Research on these packaged treatments has proliferated in the hope that individual procedures will combine to form a more powerful and comprehensive program. Moreover, a program that includes many treatment options could presumably permit the tailoring of components to important individual differences of smokers. One common vehicle used in these research efforts has been a *manual.* This document usually provides an overview of the behavioral perspective of cigarette smoking, general aspects of behavior-change technology (shaping, chaining, reward-punishment, etc.) and specific treatment prescriptions to help eliminate smoking. Some manuals have been designed to be self-administered and are completely self-contained; others are intended as aids to treatment by a consultant. Glasgow and Rosen (in press) have reviewed the use of manuals in behavior therapy, including smoking control, and have noted the need for continued development and research. *Become an Ex-Smoker* represents a carefully-reasoned package of skills in a manual format.

A number of research investigations have included self-control package procedures. Several programs are notable in reporting impressive absolute results. Brengelmann (1973) in Germany has developed a self-control package composed of up to 37 procedures: changing brands daily, limiting smoking to certain times and places, delay lighting after urges, and the like. In one study, this package emphasizing stimulus control and gradual reduction was found to be superior to various other smoking treatments, including a placebo-control condition. Subsequent investigation revealed that the self-control procedures were significantly improved on addition of contingency contracting adjunctive arrangements; fifty-eight percent of subjects were abstinent at the two-month follow-up. The program is currently under evaluation as a mail-order treatment. Although the limited follow-up precludes strong conclusions, Brengelmann's efforts suggest that self-control procedures may require an intensive treatment regimen in order to produce substantial levels of success. Brockway, Kleinmann, Edelson, and Gruenewald (1977) used a comprehensive treatment package of nonaversive procedures and obtained no significant differences between the treatment and control conditions at 12-month follow-up. Geisenger (1976) reported more optimistic results in group treatment that included intensive professional consultation; forty-eight percent of subjects were not smoking at 20 months.

Development of nonaversive procedures within a comprehensive treatment package is still in its infancy. Because it is likely that this format lends itself best to cost-effective mass-treatment applications, more intensive research effort is clearly needed.

Several studies have obtained notable success in applying self-control packages with aversion procedures. Pomerleau and Ciccone (1974) used a broad spectrum of self-control and aversion procedures and found that 46 percent of their subjects were abstinent at the 11-month follow-up. Chapman et al. (1971) used electric shock in the laboratory in conjunction with packaged self-control procedures; fifty-four percent of their subjects were abstinent at the 12-month follow-up. In the Morrow, Sachs, Gmeinder, & Burgess (1973) study, 46 percent of the subjects remained abstinent one year after a program combining rapid-smoking aversion

in the office and at home and a number of self-control procedures. Moreover, of those subjects who also participated in
group meetings following the conclusion of the intensive-
treatment phase, 90 percent were one year later.

More recent studies combining aversion and selected
self-control procedures have yielded mixed results. A few
investigators have reported considerable effectiveness
(Lando, 1977; Best et al., 1976; and Delahunt & Curran,
1976), and some have found ambiguous results (Danaher,
1977 b; Glasgow, 1977; Flaxman, in press).

The above studies are, on balance, encouraging. The
evidence, which must be taken with caution, points to the fact
that combination procedures are not always more effective
than the individual components in producing cessation. This
pattern of results is sobering, but we believe it should not
discourage further effort in this direction. Theoretical and
empirical work in behavioral self-control is still in its infancy.
As principles and procedures become refined, applications
to smoking reduction should become more effective.

The reader who has faithfully completed the section on
the treatment program and then the literature review may be
disappointed because the success rates achieved by social-
learning procedures, which form the heart of our treatment
program, are rarely better than 50 percent, and often much
less. Smoking is, as we have noted, a difficult behavior to
change. We have not pulled any punches in reviewing the
empirical literature, but we also believe there is basis for
optimism. The social-learning approach has been more systematically evaluated and has shown more promising results
than have other methods (Bernstein & McAlister, 1976; and
Lichtenstein & Danaher, 1976). Social-learning procedures
also have the virtue of being adaptable for self-
administration. The core of the social-learning approach is a
methodological commitment to systematic evaluation of

theory and technique. In this way, we expect to see further progress in behavioral approaches to smoking control.

Finally, it must be added that the research evidence may present an overly negative perspective on smoking-control efforts. The vast population of smokers who never attend smoking clinics have not contributed to the reported research literature. Yet, recent estimates suggest that millions of smokers have permanently quit on their own, without the help of special clinics or professional consultation. There is a good reason to believe, then, that smokers in the research studies may have had more tenacious smoking habits than most smokers. In developing this book, which includes the most successful treatment components available, we hope to improve the probability of successful, long-term, self-initiated attempts at quitting. Our feedback questionnaire form at the end of Chapter 11 will allow us to evaluate the effectiveness of our efforts and enable us to write an even more powerful text soon.

References

ANDREWS, D. A. *Aversive treatment procedures in the modification of smoking.* Unpublished doctoral dissertation, Queens University, Canada, 1970.

ARMITAGE, A. K. Some recent observations relating to the absorption of nicotine from tobacco smoke. In Dunn, W. L., Jr. (ed.), *Smoking behavior: Motives and incentives.* Washington, D.C.: Winston & Sons, 1973.

AXELROD, S., HALL, R. V., WEIS, L., & ROHRER, S. Use of self-imposed contingencies to reduce the frequency of smoking behavior. In Mahoney, M. J., & Thoresen, C. E. (eds.), *Self-control: Power to the person.* Monterey, Calif.: Brooks/Cole, 1974, pp. 77–85.

AZRIN, N. H., & POWELL, J. Behavioral engineering: The reduction of smoking behavior by a conditioning apparatus and procedure. *Journal of Applied Behavior Analysis,* 1968, *1,* 193–200.

BANDURA, A. *Principles of behavior modification.* New York: Holt, Rinehart & Winston, 1969.

BERECZ, J. M. Modification of smoking behaviors through self-administered punishment of imagined behavior: A new approach to aversion therapy. *Journal of Consulting and Clinical Psychology,* 1972, *38,* 244–250.

BERECZ, J. M. Smoking, stuttering, sex, and pizza: Is there commonality? Paper presented at the meeting of the Association for Advancement of Behavior Therapy, Chicago, November, 1974.

BERNARD, H. S., & EFRAN, J. S. Eliminating versus reducing smoking using pocket timers. *Behavior Research and Therapy,* 1972, *10,* 399–401.

BERNSTEIN, D. A. & MCALISTER, A. The modification of smoking behavior: Progress and problems. *Addictive Behaviors,* 1976, *1,* 89–102.

BERNSTEIN, D. A. The modification of smoking behavior: An evaluative review. *Psychological Bulletin,* 1969, *71,* 418–440.

BERNSTEIN, D. A. The modification of smoking behavior: An evaluative review. In Hunt, W. A., (ed.), *Learning mechanisms in smoking.* Chicago: Aldine, 1970.

BEST, J. A. Tailoring smoking withdrawal procedures to personality and motivational differences. *Journal of Consulting and Clinical Psychology,* 1975, *43,* 1–8.

BEST, J. A., OWEN, L. E., & TRENTADUE, L. Comparison of satiation and rapid smoking in self-managed smoking cessation. *Addictive Behaviors,* in press.

BORNSTEIN, P. H., CARMODY, T. P., RELINGER, H., ZOHN, J. C., DEVINE, D. A., & BUGGE, I. D. *Reduction of smoking behavior through token reinforcement procedures.* Unpublished manuscript, University of Montana, 1975.

BRENGELMANN, J. C. *Verbesserte methoden zur behandlung des rauchens.* Unpublished manuscript, 1973. (Available from Max Planck Institute fur Psychiatrie, Department of Psychology, Kraepelinstrasse 10, D-8, Munchen 40, Federal Republic of Germany.)

BROCKWAY, B. S., KLEINMANN, G., EDELSON, J., & GRUENEWALD, K. Nonaversive procedures and their effects on cigarette smoking: A clinical group study. *Addictive Behaviors*, 1977, *2*, 121–128.

CAUTELA, J. R. Treatment of smoking by covert sensitization. *Psychological Reports*, 1970, *26*, 415–420.

CHAPMAN, R. R., SMITH, J. W., & LAYDEN, T. A. Elimination of cigarette smoking by punishment and self-management training. *Behavior Research and Therapy*, 1971, *9*, 255–264.

CLAIBORN, W. L., LEWIS, P., & HUMBLE, S. Stimulus satiation and smoking: A revisit. *Journal of Consulting Psychology*, 1972, *28*, 416–419.

CONWAY, J. B. Behavioral self-control through aversive conditioning and self-management. *Journal of Consulting and Clinical Psychology*, 1977, *45*, 348–357.

DANAHER, B. G. Coverant control of cigarette smoking. In Krumboltz, J. D. and Thoresen, C. E.(eds.), *Counseling methods.* New York: Holt, Rinehart, and Winston, 1976, pp. 117–124.

DANAHER, B. G. Research on rapid smoking: Interim summary and recommendations. *Addictive Behaviors*, 1977, *2*, 151–166 (a).

DANAHER, B. G. Rapid smoking and self-control in the modification of smoking behavior. *Journal of Consulting and Clinical Psychology*, 1977, *45*, 1068–1075(b).

DANAHER, B. G., & LICHTENSTEIN, E. Aversion therapy issues: A note of clarification. *Behavior Therapy*, 1974, *5*, 112–116 (a).

DANAHER, B. G., & LICHTENSTEIN, E. An experimental analysis of coverant control: Cuing and consequence. Paper presented at the meeting of the Western Psychological Association, San Francisco, April 1974. (b)

DELAHUNT, J., & CURRAN, J. P. Effectiveness of negative practice and self-control techniques in the reduction of smoking behavior. *Journal of Consulting and Clinical Psychology*, 1976, *44*, 1002–1007.

DERICCO, A., BRIGHAM, A., & GARLINGTON, K. Development and evaluation of treatment paradigms for the suppression of smoking behavior. *Journal of Applied Behavior Analysis*, 1977, *10*, 173–181.

ELLIOTT, R., & TIGHE, T. Breaking the cigarette habit: Effects of a technique involving threatened loss of money. *Psychological Record*, 1968, *18*, 503–513.

FLAXMAN, J. Quitting smoking now or later: Gradual, abrupt, delayed and immediate quitting. *Behavior Therapy*, in press.

FREDERIKSEN, L. W., PETERSON, G. L., & MURPHY, W. D. Controlled smoking development and maintenance. *Addictive Behaviors*, 1976, *1*, 193–196.

FREDERIKSEN, L. W., & PETERSON, G. L. Controlled smoking: The case for a new treatment goal. Paper presented at the Association for the Advancement of Behavior Therapy, New York, December 1976.

FUHRER, R. E. The effects of covert sensitization with relaxation induction, covert sensitization without relaxation instructions, and attention-placebo on the reduction of cigarette smoking. Unpublished doctoral dissertation, University of Montana, 1971. *Dissertation Abstracts International*, 1972, *32*, 6644B–6645B. (University Microfilms No. 72-13, 449).

GEISENGER, D. L. A broad-range program to eliminate cigarette smoking. In Krumboltz, J. D., & Thoresen, C. E. (eds.), *Counseling methods*. New York: Holt, Rinehart and Winston, 1976, pp. 124–137.

GLASGOW, R. E. *The effects of a self-control manual and amount of therapist contact in the modification of smoking behavior.* Unpublished doctoral dissertation, University of Oregon, 1977.

GLASGOW, R. E., & ROSEN, G. M. Behavioral bibliotherapy: A review of self-help behavior therapy manuals. *Psychological Bulletin*, in press.

GORDON, S. B. Self-control with a covert aversive stimulus: Modification of smoking. Unpublished doctoral dissertation, West Virginia University, 1971. *Dissertation Abstracts International*, 1972, *32*, 4858B–4859B. (University Microfilms No. 72–5154).

GUTMANN, M., & MARSTON, A. R. Problems of *S*'s motivation in a behavioral program for reduction of cigarette smoking. *Psychological Reports*, 1967, *20*, 1107–1114.

HARK, R. D. An examination of the effectiveness of coverant conditioning in the reduction of cigarette smoking. Unpublished doctoral dissertation, Michigan State University, 1970. *Dissertation Abstracts International*, 1970, *31*, 2958B. (University Microfilms No. 70–20).

HARRIS, D. E., & LICHTENSTEIN, E. Contribution of nonspecific social variables to a successful behavioral treatment of smoking. Paper presented at the meeting of the Western Psychological Association, San Francisco, April, 1971.

HARRIS, M. B., & ROTHBERG, C. A self-control approach to reducing smoking. *Psychological Reports*, 1972, *31*, 165–166.

HOMME, L. E. Perspectives in psychology, XXIV: Control of coverants, the operants of the mind. *Psychological Record*, 1965, *15*, 501–511.

HUNT, W. A., & BESPALEC, D. A. An evaluation of current methods of modifying smoking behavior. *Journal of Clinical Psychology*, 1974, *30*, 431–438.

HUTCHINSON, R. R., & EMLEY, G. S. Effects of nicotine on avoidance, conditioned suppression and aggression response measures in animals and man. In Dunn, W. L., Jr. (ed.), *Smoking behavior: Motives and incentives*. Washington, D.C.: Winston & Sons, 1973.

JANIS, I. L., & HOFFMANN, D. Facilitating effects of daily contact between partners who make a decision to cut down on smoking. *Journal of Personality and Social Psychology*, 1970, *17*, 25–35.

JARVIK, M. E. Further observations on nicotine as the reinforcing agent in smoking. In W. L. Dunn, Jr. (ed.), *Smoking behavior: Motives and incentives*. Washington, D. C.: Winston & Sons, 1973.

JOHNSON, S. S. The evaluation of self-control techniques upon differing types of smoking behavior. Unpublished dissertation, University of Colorado, 1968. *Dissertation Abstracts International*, 1969, *29*, 3507B. (University Microfilms No. 69–4370).

KAREN, R. L., & BOGARDUS, L. C. *A study of the short-term and long-term effectiveness of a self-control procedure for smoking control.* Unpublished manuscript, California State University, 1973.

KEUTZER, C. S. Behavior modification of smoking: The experimental investigation of diverse techniques. *Behavior Research and Therapy*, 1968, *6*, 137–157.

KOPEL, S. A. The effects of self-control, booster sessions, and cognitive factors on the maintenance of smoking reduction. Unpublished doctoral dissertation, University of Oregon, 1974. *Dissertation Abstracts International*, 1975, *35*, 4182B–4183B. (University Microfilms No. 75–3895).

LANDO, H. A. Aversive conditioning and contingency management in the treatment of smoking. *Journal of Consulting and Clinical Psychology*, 1976, *44*, 312.

LANDO, H. A. A comparison of excessive and rapid smoking in the modification of chronic smoking behavior. *Journal of Consulting and Clinical Psychology*, 1975, *43*, 350–355.

LANDO, H. A. Successful treatment of smokers with a broad-spectrum behavioral approach. *Journal of Consulting and Clinical Psychology*, 1977, *45*, 361–366.

LAWSON, D. M., & MAY, R. B. Three procedures for the extinction of smoking behavior. *Psychological Record*, 1970, *20*, 151–157.

LEVINE, B. A. Effectiveness of contingent and noncontingent electric shock in reducing cigarette smoking. *Psychological Reports*, 1974, *34*, 223–226.

LEVINSON, B. L., SHAPIRO, D., SCHWARTZ, G. E., & TURSKY, B. Smoking elimination by gradual reduction. *Behavior Therapy*, 1971, *2*, 477–487.

LICHTENSTEIN, E., & DANAHER, B. G. Modification of smoking behavior: A critical analysis of theory, research, and practice. In Hersen, M., Eisler, R. M., & Miller, P. M. (eds.), *Progress in behavior modification* (vol. 3). New York: Academic Press, 1976, pp. 70–132.

LICHTENSTEIN, E., HARRIS, D. E., BIRCHLER, G. R., WAHL, J. M., & SCHMAHL, D. P. Comparison of rapid smoking, warm, smoky air, and attention placebo in the modification of smoking behavior. *Journal of Consulting and Clinical Psychology*, 1973, *40*, 92–98.

LICHTENSTEIN, E., & GLASGOW, R. E. Rapid smoking: Side effects and safeguards. *Journal of Consulting and Clinical Psychology*, 1977, *45*, 815–821.

LICHTENSTEIN, E., & KEUTZER, C. S. Modification of smoking behavior: A later look. In Rubin, R. D., Fensterheim, H., Lazarus, A.A., and Franks, C. M. (eds.), *Advances in behavior therapy*. New York: Academic Press, 1971.

LUBLIN, I., & BARRY, J. Aversive counter-conditioning of cigarette addiction. Paper presented at the meeting of the Western Psychological Association, Anaheim, Calif., April 1973.

LUBLIN, I., & JOSLYN, L. Aversive conditioning of cigarette addiction. Paper presented at the meeting of the Western Psychological Association, Los Angeles, September 1968.

MAHONEY, M. J. *Cognition and behavior modification*. Boston: Ballinger Press, 1974.

MARSTON, A. R., & FELDMAN, S. E. Toward the use of self-control in behavior modification. *Journal of Consulting and Clinical Psychology*, 1972, *39*, 429–433.

MARSTON, A. R., & MCFALL, R. M. Comparison of behavior modification approaches to smoking reduction. *Journal of Consulting and Clinical Psychology*, 1971, *36*, 153–162.

MCCALLUM, R. N. The modification of cigarette smoking behavior: A comparison of treatment techniques. Paper presented at the meeting of the Southwestern Psychological Association, San Antonio, Tex., April 1971.

MCFALL, R. M., & HAMMEN, C. L. Motivation, structure, and self-monitoring: Role of nonspecific factors in smoking reduction. *Journal of Consulting and Clinical Psychology*, 1971, *37*, 80–86.

MILLER, A., & GIMPL, M. Operant conditioning and self-control of smoking and studying. *Journal of Genetic Psychology*, 1971, *119*, 181–186.

MILLER, W. R., & MUÑOZ, R. F. *How to control your drinking.* Englewood Cliffs, N. J.: Prentice-Hall, 1976.

MORROW, J. E., SACHS, L. B., GMEINDER, S., & BURGESS, H. Elimination of cigarette smoking behavior by stimulus satiation, self-control techniques, and group therapy. Paper presented at the meeting of the Western Psychological Association, Anaheim, Calif., April 1973.

NEHEMKIS, A. M., & LICHTENSTEIN, E. Conjoint social reinforcement in the treatment of smoking. Paper presented at the meeting of the Western Psychological Association, San Francisco, April 1971.

NOLAN, J. D. Self-control procedures in the modification of smoking behavior. *Journal of Consulting and Clinical Psychology*, 1968, *32*, 92–93.

OBER, D. C. Modification of smoking behavior. *Journal of Consulting and Clinical Psychology*, 1968, *32*, 543–549.

POMERLEAU, O. F., & CICCONE, P. Preliminary results of a treatment program for smoking cessation using multiple behavior modification techniques. Paper presented at the meeting of the Association for Advancement of Behavior Therapy, Chicago, November 1974.

POWELL, J. R., & AZRIN, N. The effects of shock as a punisher for cigarette smoking. *Journal of Applied Behavior Analysis*, 1968, *1*, 63–71.

RESNICK, J. H. The control of smoking by stimulus satiation. *Behavior Research and Therapy*, 1968, *6*, 113–114. (a)

RESNICK, J. H. Effects of stimulus satiation on the overlearned maladaptive response of cigarette smoking. *Journal of Consulting and Clinical Psychology*, 1968, *32*, 501–505. (b)

ROBERTS, A. H. Self-control procedures in the modification of smoking behavior: Replication. *Psychological Reports*, 1969, *24*, 675–676.

RUSSELL, M. A. H. Tobacco smoking and nicotine dependence. In Gibbons, R. J., Israel, Y., Kalent, H., Popham, R. E., Schmidt, W., and Smart, R. G. (eds.), *Research advances in alcohol and drug problems (vol. 3)*. New York: Wiley, 1976, pp. 1–47.

RUSSELL, M. A. H. Effect of electrical aversion on cigarette smoking. *British Medical Journal*, 1970, *1*, 82–86.

RUSSELL, M. A. H., ARMSTRONG, E., & PATEL, U. A. The role of temporal contiguity in electric aversion therapy for cigarette smoking: Analysis of behavior changes. *Behavior Research and Therapy*, 1976, *14*, 103–123.

RUTNER, I. T. *The modification of smoking behavior through techniques of self-control*. Unpublished master's thesis, Wichita State University, 1967.

SACHS, L. B., BEAN, H., & MORROW, J. E. Comparison of smoking treatments. *Behavior Therapy*, 1970, *1*, 465–472.

SCHACHTER, S., SILVERSTEIN, B., KOZLOWZKI, L. T., PERLICK, D., HERMAN, C. P., & LIEBLING, B. Studies of the interaction of psychological and pharmacological determinants of smoking. *Journal of Experimental Psychology: General*, 1977, *106*, 3–40.

SCHMAHL, D. P., LICHTENSTEIN, E., & HARRIS, D. E. Successful treatment of habitual smokers with warm, smoky air and rapid smoking. *Journal of Consulting and Clinical Psychology*, 1972, *38*, 105–111.

SHAPIRO, D., TURSKY, B., SCHWARTZ, G. E., & SCHNIDMAN, S. K. Smoking on cue: A behavioral approach to smoking reduction. *Journal of Health and Social Behavior*, 1971, *12*, 108–113.

SIPICH, J. F., RUSSELL, R. K., & TOBIAS, L. L. A comparison of covert sensitization and "nonspecific" treatment in the modification of smoking behavior. *Journal of Behavior Therapy and Experimental Psychiatry*, 1974, *5*, 201–203.

SPRING, F. L., SIPICH, J. F., TRIMBLE, R. W., & GOECKNER, D. J. Effects of contingency and noncontingency contracts in the context of a self-control-oriented smoking modification program. *Behavior Therapy*, in press.

STEFFY, R. A., MEICHENBAUM, D., & BEST, A. J. Aversive and cognitive factors in the modification of smoking behavior. *Behavior Research and Therapy*, 1970, *8*, 115–126.

ST. PIERRE, R., & LAWRENCE, P. S. Smoking modification: The effects of combining positive and aversive treatment and maintenance procedures. Paper presented at the meeting of the Association for Advancement of Behavior Therapy, Chicago, November 1974.

SUSHINSKY, L. W. Expectation of future treatment, stimulus satiation, and smoking. *Journal of Consulting and Clinical Psychology*, 1972, *39*, 343.

THORESEN, C. E., & MAHONEY, M. J. *Behavioral self-control.* New York: Holt, Rinehart and Winston, 1974.

TIGHE, T. J., & ELLIOTT, R. A. A technique for controlling behavior in natural life settings. *Journal of Applied Behavior Analysis*, 1968, *1*, 263–266.

TOOLEY, J. T., & PRATT, S. An experimental procedure for extinction of smoking behavior. *Psychological Record*, 1967, *17*, 209–218.

UPPER, D, & MEREDITH, L. *A timed-interval procedure for modifying cigarette-smoking behavior.* Unpublished manuscript, Veterans Administration Hospital, Brockton, Mass., 1971.

VOGLER, R. E., LUNDE, S. E., JOHNSON, G. R., & MARTIN, P. L. Electrical aversion conditioning with chronic alcoholics. *Journal of Consulting and Clinical Psychology*, 1970, *34*, 302–307.

WAGNER, M. K., & BRAGG, R. A. Comparing behavior modification approaches to habit decrement—smoking. *Journal of Consulting and Clinical Psychology*, 1970, *34*, 258–263.

WATSON, D. L., & THARP, R. G. *Self-directed behavior: Self-modification for personal adjustment.* Monterey, Calif.: Brooks/Cole, 1972.

WEINROBE, P. A., & LICHTENSTEIN, E. The use of urges as termination criterion in a rapid smoking program for habitual smokers. Paper presented at the meeting of the Western Psychological Association, Sacramento, April 1975.

WEISS, J. I. An experimental examination of Cautela's covert sensitization as a smoking reduction technique. Unpublished doctoral dissertation, University of North Dakota, 1974. *Dissertation Abstracts International*, 1974, *35*, 2454B. (University Microfilms No. 74–24, 540).

WILSON, G. T., & DAVISON, G. C. Aversion techniques in behavior therapy: Some theoretical and metatheoretical considerations, *Journal of Consulting and Clinical Psychology*, 1969, *33*, 327–329.

WINETT, R. A. Parameters of deposit contracts in the modification of smoking. *Psychological Record*, 1973, *23*, 49–60.

WISOCKI, P. A., & ROONEY, E. J. A comparison of thought stopping and covert sensitization techniques in the treatment of smoking: A brief report. *Psychological Record*, 1974, *24*, 191–192.

Index

SUBJECT INDEX

AUTHOR INDEX